Women and Minority Faculty in the Academic Workplace

Recruitment, Retention, and Academic Culture

Adalberto Aguirre, Jr.

ASHE-ERIC Higher Education Report Volume 27, Number 6
Adrianna J. Kezar, Series Editor

Prepared and published by

JOSSEY-BASS
A Wiley Company
San Francisco

In cooperation with

ERIC Clearinghouse on Higher Education
The George Washington University
URL: www.eriche.org

Association for the Study
of Higher Education
URL: www.tiger.coe.missouri.edu/~ashe

Graduate School of Education and Hum
The George Washington University
URL: www.gwu.edu

D1165129

Women and Minority Faculty in the Academic Workplace:
Recruitment, Retention, and Academic Culture
Adalberto Aguirre, Jr.
ASHE-ERIC Higher Education Report Volume 27, Number 6
Adrianna J. Kezar, Series Editor

This publication was prepared partially with funding from the
Office of Educational Research and Improvement, U.S.
Department of Education, under contract no. ED-99-00-0036.
The opinions expressed in this report do not necessarily re-
flect the positions or policies of OERI or the Department.

ISSN 0884-0040   ISBN 0-7879-5574-4

The ASHE-ERIC Higher Education Report is part of the
Jossey-Bass Higher and Adult Education Series and is pub-
lished eight times a year by Jossey-Bass, 350 Sansome Street,
San Francisco, California 94104-1342.

For subscription information, see the Back Issue/
Subscription Order Form in the back of this journal.

Prospective authors are strongly encouraged to contact
Adrianna Kezar, Director, ERIC Clearinghouse on Higher
Education, at (202) 296-2597 ext. 14 or akezar@eric-he-edu.

Visit the Jossey-Bass Web site at www.josseybass.com.

Printed in the United States of America on acid-free recycled
paper containing 100 percent recovered waste paper, of
which at least 20 percent is postconsumer waste.

EXECUTIVE SUMMARY

Institutions of higher education have attempted to diversify their faculty by recruiting women and minorities. Those efforts, however, have been implemented without understanding how women and minority faculty fit in an institution dominated by men, especially White men. In particular, recruitment has taken place without an understanding of the social forces that shape the professional socialization and workplace satisfaction of women and minority faculty. The use of affirmative action in academia to increase the representation of women and minority faculty, for example, has often resulted in workers' perception that they are tokens or outcomes of reverse discrimination practiced on White men. By no means is the term *minority faculty* in this monograph used to identify a homogeneous population. Rather, the term is used as a descriptive category to discuss the workplace experiences of non-White faculty. As such, the term *minority faculty* includes Latinos, Blacks, Asians, and American Indians. It is not possible to examine the workplace experiences of each minority group, given the limits of the research literature. In particular, the research literature on minority faculty focuses primarily on the experiences of Latinos and Blacks. The research literature does not so much omit Asian and American Indian faculty from study as it recognizes its limitations in making substantive comparisons between minority groups. That is, more information is simply available on Black and Latino faculty than on Asian or American Indian faculty. As a result, comparisons between the groups run the risk of being conceptually weak, given a lack of data and information for some of the groups. In an attempt to address the need for substantive comparisons in the minority faculty population, this monograph examines the relative differences between minority groups in the faculty population when the data permit comparisons.

The term *women faculty,* on the one hand, is a descriptive category that includes women's experiences in the workplace. The term is used to discuss and contrast the academic experiences of women and men faculty in the workplace. On the other hand, the term is not homogeneous in its use; in particular, the term is not designed to bury the workplace experiences of minority women faculty. To this end, the workplace experiences of minority and White women faculty are compared and contrasted to identify commonalities and differences between them. In this manner, the understanding of how *minority status* and *gender* are associated with the workplace experiences of minority women faculty are enhanced.

What Is the Status of Women and Minority Faculty in Academia?

The number of women and minority faculty in higher education has been increasing, with the implementation of affirmative action initiatives in higher education serving as a vehicle for increasing their representation. Despite the increased numbers, however, women and minority faculty remain underrepresented in higher education relative to their numbers in the U.S. population. Moreover, despite appreciable gains in the number of Ph.D. degrees earned by women and minorities, their proportionate representation in the U.S. faculty population has remained unchanged.

What Are the Organizational Features of the Academic Workplace?

The academic workplace is characterized in popular thinking as a place of enlightened thought and discourse that is immune to influences from the outside world. Its perceived immunity to the outside world has resulted in a perception that the academic workplace is free of conflict and stress. The reality, however, is that the academic workplace is characterized by group struggles over the definition of knowledge and about what it means to be a knowledgeable person. To survive in the academic workplace, faculty members must align themselves with and participate in institutional networks that define one's position in a knowledge hierarchy.

How are Women and Minority Faculty Treated in the Academic Workplace?

The academic workplace has been described as *chilly* and *alienating* for women and minority faculty. On the one hand, women and minority faculty find themselves burdened with heavy teaching and service responsibilities that constrain their opportunity to engage in research and publication. On the other hand, women and minority faculty are expected to assume and perform institutional roles that allow higher education institutions to pursue diversity on campus. But those roles are ignored in the faculty reward system, especially the awarding of tenure. The academic workplace is thus *chilly* and *alienating* for women and minority faculty because they are ascribed a peripheral role in the academic workplace and are expected to perform roles that are in conflict with expectations.

What Barriers to Professional Socialization Do Women and Minority Faculty Experience in the Academic Workplace?

Women and minority faculty are less satisfied than White male faculty with the workplace because women and minority faculty perceive themselves to be the victims of salary inequities and a biased reward system. Women and minority faculty are also perceived in the academic workplace as less competent than White male faculty. As a result, White male faculty often discredit feminist and minority research. Women and minority faculty face barriers in the academic workplace that question their legitimacy as academics and their access to institutional resources and rewards that promote professional socialization.

Why Do We Need to Study the Academic Workplace for Women and Minority Faculty?

An examination of the academic workplace for women and minority faculty becomes imperative if one considers that demographic predictions suggest that the U.S. workforce will become increasingly diverse in the 21st century. The two populations most likely to determine diversity in the workplace in the 21st century are women and minorities. An increased representation of women and minorities in the workplace has implications for institutions of higher education, especially at a time when it appears that faculty pools are shrinking as the demand for new faculty is increasing. As a result, one may speculate that women and minorities will increase their representation in the faculty population, thus providing institutions of higher education with an enhanced opportunity to diversify their faculty ranks. If women and minority faculty are going to increase their *representativeness* in higher education, it is necessary to examine the academic workplace to understand how women and minority faculty fit in the academic culture.

CONTENTS

Foreword   ix

Acknowledgments   xi

The Status of Women and Minority Faculty: **1**
Changing or Unchanging?
Changes in the Faculty Population   2
Changes in Faculty Ranks   5
Doctoral Degrees and Faculty Representation   9
A Matter of Representativeness   12
Minority Faculty   15
Summary   17

The Academic Workplace   **19**
Images of Academe   20
Academic Culture   23
The Relationship Between Academic Culture   27
    and the Academic Workplace
Diversity in Academia and the Academic Workplace   31
Summary   36

The Academic Workplace for Women   **39**
and Minority Faculty
Issues in the Workplace for Women Faculty   40
Minority Women Faculty   42
Issues in the Workplace for Minority Faculty   44
The Institutional Context   46
Fitting In in the Academic Workplace   50
Organizational Fit   53
Summary   56

Issues Facing Women and Minority Faculty   **57**
Barriers in the Academic Workplace   58
Workplace Issues   60
Professional Socialization   69
Negotiated Identities   72
Summary   74

Summary Observations and Suggestions   **75**
Diversifying the Faculty   75
Academic Culture and Diversity   79
The Academic Workplace and Diversity   81
Professional Socialization of Women and   84
    Minority Faculty
A Final Note   86

References	**91**
Name Index	**111**
Subject Index	**121**
ASHE-ERIC Higher Education Reports	**125**
Advisory Board	126
Consulting Editors and Review Panel	127
Recent Titles	128
Order Form	

FOREWORD

Each year the American Council of Education publishes a status report on minorities in higher education, examining the representation of students, faculty, staff, and administrators. These reports illustrate a slow increase in the number of minorities and women in the academy. Yet after many years of affirmative action and active recruitment, many individuals believe that the increase in minority representation, in particular, is far behind reaching an equitable level. The number of minority faculty has been slow to increase, especially in certain disciplines such as law, engineering, math, and other sciences. If the number of minority faculty does not increase, students are left without role models of different races and genders. Possible reasons for and solutions to this situation emerge in one article or report after another. This monograph synthesizes what we know from 10 years of research about issues that are impacting campuses' ability to recruit, retain, and create an inclusive environment for minorities and women faculty. It also adds new dimensions to our understanding by examining professional socialization and tenure for women and minority faculty. These processes aim at making faculty part of the "culture of the academy," but it is professional socialization and tenure where cultural conflict can often be ignited.

Adalberto Aguirre, professor of sociology at the University of California–Riverside, has been examining why recruitment of minority and women faculty has fallen short. Aguirre's previous monograph for the ASHE-ERIC higher education series, *Chicanos in Higher Education,* examines the undergraduate experience, patterns of enrollment, and career paths for Chicanos. The current work builds on his earlier scholarship, detailing how recruitment has failed to examine the academic culture for underrepresented faculty. In particular, how does the institutional environment affect the retention and future recruitment of underrepresented faculty? For example, if the institutional environment in academia is hostile for underrepresented faculty, they may leave for other positions or tell others about their experiences, dissuading others from pursuing a career in academia.

The academic environment was first described as *chilly* for women in the 1970s, and the metaphor remains true for many women and minority faculty. Aguirre deconstructs the popular and often misguided notion of the academy as a place of peace, equality, truth, and the life of the mind. At

THE STATUS OF WOMEN AND MINORITY FACULTY: Changing or Unchanging?

Postsecondary education institutions have been deliberately slow in recruiting minority persons and women into their faculty ranks. The limited presence of women and minority faculty in academia has reduced their opportunity to an increasingly important part of higher education and to achieve equity with White male faculty (Aguirre, 1995a; Fields, 1988; Hayes, 1990; Stecklein and Lorenz, 1986). The limited presence of women and minority faculty in academia will become even more apparent in the 21st century—a century in which women and minority persons are expected to become more noticeable in the U.S. population (Finkelstein, 1984; Gummer, 1998; Maxson and Hair, 1990; Tack and Patitu, 1992). For example, although the number of women enrolling in colleges and universities during the 1980s increased noticeably, the number of women entering the faculty ranks remained relatively unchanged (Vandell and Fishbein, 1989).

The 1990s witnessed a similar pattern: Women and minorities increased their numbers attending colleges and universities but made only marginal progress in increasing their numbers in the faculty ranks (Carter and O'Brien, 1993; Ottinger and Sikula, 1993). Although affirmative action has been portrayed as a vehicle for increasing the number of women and minority faculty in academia, it has not enhanced their representation in the faculty ranks (Aguirre, 1997; Higgerson and Higgerson, 1991). According to Johnsrud and Sadao (1998), the increase of minority faculty during the 1980s and early 1990s has been negligible. Similarly, Riger, Stokes, Raja, and Sullivan (1997) observed that although the number of women students in higher education increased dramatically during the 1980s the number of women faculty did not. Even though they became the "majority" of the undergraduate enrollment in institutions of higher education during the 1990s, women have not fared well in academia despite the passage of antidiscrimination laws starting in 1972: "Women have yet to enjoy the benefits and pleasures of academic life to the same level and degree as presently experienced by men . . . despite the fact that women perform better than men in all fields and at all levels of the educational ladder" (Billard, 1994, p. 115).

Women and minorities entering the faculty ranks often find a *chilly* and *unreceptive* environment. The use of

Although affirmative action has been portrayed as a vehicle for increasing the number of women and minority faculty in academia, it has not enhanced their representation in the faculty ranks.

affirmative action initiatives, for example, to increase the representation of women and minorities in the faculty ranks has facilitated the emergence of an organizational culture that is cold and indifferent toward women and minorities. Reyes and Halcon (1991) note that although "the implementation of affirmative action programs provided more access to minorities," they "left all minority professionals and academics with a legacy of tokenism— a stigma that has been difficult to dispel" (p. 173). Similarly, Heilman (1994) observes that affirmative action creates a "stigma of incompetence" for a woman perceived to have "benefited from affirmative action policies" (153). Ironically, affirmative action initiatives that were designed to increase the representation of women and minorities in the faculty ranks have resulted in an environment in academia that isolates rather than incorporates women and minorities in the academic culture. The purpose of this section is to construct a descriptive portrait of women and minority faculty in academia that helps us discuss their *representativeness* in academia.

Changes in the Faculty Population
The faculty population in U.S. institutions of higher education increased 18% between 1980 and 1993. There were 452,300 persons in the faculty populations in 1980 and 531,800 in 1993 (National Center for Education Statistics, 1986, 1996). According to Table 1, women increased their number in the faculty population by 53.5% between 1980 and 1993, while men increased their number 5.1%. Women in the faculty population also enhanced their proportionate representation in the faculty population from 25.8% in 1980 to 33.6% in 1993. Despite the appreciable increase of women in the faculty population between 1980 and 1993, however, men account for the majority of the faculty population. For example, there were nearly twice as many men as women in the faculty population in 1993.

Regardless of race or ethnic background, women increased their number more than men in the faculty population between 1980 and 1993 (Table 1). White women increased their number in the faculty population by 50.5% between 1980 and 1993, Black women by 33.3%, Latinas by 150%, Asian women by 200%, and American Indian women by 60%. As impressive as the increase in the number of

TABLE 1

Faculty by Sex, Race, and Ethnicity, 1980 and 1993*

	1980		1993		Change
Population	*N*	*%*	*N*	*%*	*1980–1993*
Total	452.3	100.0	531.8	100.0	17.6%
Men	335.8	74.2	353.0	66.4	5.1%
Women	116.5	25.8	178.8	33.6	53.5%
White	411.0	100.0	468.0	100.0	13.9%
Men	308.0	74.9	313.0	66.9	1.6%
Women	103.0	25.1	155.0	33.1	50.5%
Black	20.0	100.0	25.0	100.0	25.0%
Men	11.0	55.0	13.0	52.0	18.2%
Women	9.0	45.0	12.0	48.0	33.3%
Latino	7.0	100.0	12.0	100.0	71.4%
Men	5.0	71.4	7.0	58.3	40.0%
Women	2.0	28.6	5.0	41.7	150.0%
Asian	13.0	100.0	25.0	100.0	92.3%
Men	11.0	84.6	19.0	76.0	72.7%
Women	2.0	15.4	6.0	24.0	200.0%
Am. Ind.	1.3	100.0	1.8	100.0	38.5%
Men	.8	61.5	1.0	55.6	25.0%
Women	.5	38.5	.8	44.4	60.0%

* Full-time instructional staff; number in thousands.

Source: National Center for Education Statistics, 1986, 1996.

minority women faculty between 1980 and 1993 appears, however, the increase was marginal compared with the increase for White women faculty. For example, according to Figure 1, White women accounted for 23% of the faculty population in 1980 and 29% in 1993. In contrast, minority women accounted for 3% of the faculty population in 1980 and 4% in 1993. Comparatively speaking, the representativeness of White women faculty increased 6 percentage points between 1980 and 1993, while it increased 1 percentage point for minority women faculty. The disparity in gains between White and minority women faculty in academia has caused some to observe that White women have benefited more from affirmative action initiatives than minority women (Bernstein and Cock, 1994).

With regard to the increase of men in the faculty population between 1980 and 1993, White men increased their number by 1.6%, Black men by 18.2%, Latinos

FIGURE 1

Representation of Men and Women in the Faculty Population, 1980 and 1993

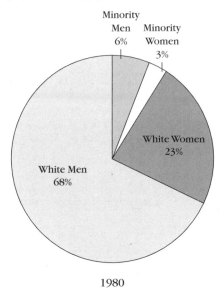

Minority Men 6%
Minority Women 3%
White Women 23%
White Men 68%

1980

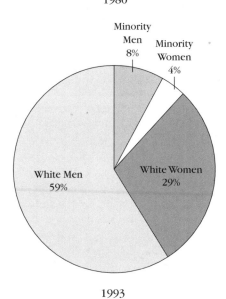

Minority Men 8%
Minority Women 4%
White Women 29%
White Men 59%

1993

by 40.0%, Asian men by 72.7%, and American Indian men by 25.0% (Table 1). Minority men accounted for 6% of the faculty population in 1980, 7.5% in 1993 (Figure 1). The representativeness of minority men faculty thus increased 1.5 percentage points between 1980 and 1993. Moreover, the increase in the number of minority men faculty between 1980 and 1993 was comparable to the increase in the number of minority women faculty in the same time period. Ironically, compared with the increase of White women in the faculty population between 1980 and 1993, minority men did not fare as well. According to Cortese (1992), the disparity in gains between White women faculty and minority men faculty suggests that affirmative action programs have benefited White women more than minority men.

Changes in Faculty Ranks
Tables 2 and 3 summarize the representation of men and women, by race and ethnicity, in the various faculty ranks for 1981 and 1993. By way of comparison, Asian men and women had the most noticeable gains in faculty ranks between 1981 and 1993, both White men and women the smallest. In general, Black, Latino, and Asian faculty had noticeable gains across the faculty ranks between 1981 and 1993, while American Indians made negligible gains. For example, an examination of the relative differences in the faculty population between 1980 and 1993 by academic rank, race, ethnicity, and sex shows that the largest increase in the number of faculty between 1981 and 1993 was at the rank of professor. Latino men had the largest increase (80%) at the rank of professor, followed by Asian men (77.1%), black men (76.5%), American Indian men (50%), and white men (22%). Latino women also had the largest increase (200%) at the rank of professor, followed by Asian women (166.7%), white women (119.6%), black women (114.3%), and American Indian women (no change).

Asian men made the largest gain in the faculty ranks (61.5%) between 1981 and 1993, followed by Latino men (56.3%), American Indian men (50.0%), black men (34.0%), and white men (3.2%). Similarly, Asian women had the largest gains in the faculty ranks (125%), followed by Latino women (119%), American Indian women (60%), white women (45.6%), and black women (44.7%).

TABLE 2

Men Faculty by Race, Ethnicity, and Academic Rank, 1981 and 1993*

	All Ranks	Professor	Associate Professor	Assistant Professor	Instructor	Lecturer
White						
1981	303.5	97.0	77.3	66.3	41.9	4.3
1993	313.3	118.3	74.2	59.7	28.8	5.5
Percent Change**	3.2	22.0	−4.0	−10.0	−31.3	27.9
Black						
1981	10.0	1.7	2.3	2.7	2.3	0.2
1993	13.4	3.0	3.1	3.8	2.1	0.4
Percent Change	34.0	76.5	34.8	40.7	−8.7	100.0
Latino						
1981	4.8	1.0	1.1	1.2	1.2	0.1
1993	7.5	1.8	1.6	1.9	1.2	0.2
Percent Change	56.3	80.0	45.5	58.3		100.0
Asian						
1981	11.7	3.5	2.7	3.4	0.9	0.2
1993	18.9	6.2	4.4	5.3	1.1	0.3
Percent Change	61.5	77.1	63.0	55.9	22.2	50.0
American Indian						
1981	0.8	0.2	0.2	0.2	0.2	a
1993	1.2	0.3	0.2	0.2	0.4	a
Percent Change	50.0	50.0	b	b	100.0	b

* Full-time instructional staff, number in thousands.

** % change (1981–1993)

a: Less than 100.

b: No change.

Source: National Center for Education Statistics, 1986, 1996.

Despite the increase of minority men and women in the faculty ranks between 1981 and 1993 noted in Tables 2 and 3, they made marginal gains in their proportionate representation at each faculty rank between 1980 and 1993. In some cases, the proportionate representation decreased. For example, despite an increase of 61.5% for Asian men in faculty ranks between 1980 and 1993 (Table 2), their proportionate representation in faculty ranks actually decreased between 1980 and 1993, from 5.8% to 5.3% (Table 4).

TABLE 3

Women Faculty by Race, Ethnicity, and Academic Rank, 1981 and 1993*

	All Ranks	Professor	Associate Professor	Assistant Professor	Instructor	Lecturer
White						
1981	106.8	10.7	19.7	32.9	30.5	3.2
1993	155.5	23.5	31.8	45.4	28.1	5.8
Percent Change**	45.6	119.6	61.4	38.0	−7.9	81.3
Black						
1981	8.5	0.7	1.3	2.7	2.8	0.2
1993	12.3	1.5	2.2	3.9	2.6	0.5
Percent Change	44.7	114.3	69.2	44.4	−7.1	150.0
Latino						
1981	2.1	0.2	0.3	0.6	0.7	0.1
1993	4.6	0.6	0.7	1.4	1.0	0.2
Percent Change	119.0	200.0	133.3	133.3	42.9	100.0
Asian						
1981	2.8	0.3	0.5	1.0	0.6	0.1
1993	6.3	0.8	1.1	2.3	1.0	0.3
Percent Change	125.0	166.7	120.0	130.0	66.7	200.0
American Indian						
1981	0.5	a	0.2	0.1	0.1	a
1993	0.8	a	0.1	0.2	0.2	a
Percent Change	60.0	b	−50.0	100.0	100.0	b

* Full-time instructional staff, number in thousands.
** % change (1981–1993)
a: Less than 100.
b: No change.
Source: National Center for Education Statistics, 1986, 1996.

Similarly, despite an increase of 125% for Asian women in the faculty ranks between 1980 and 1993, their proportionate representation in faculty ranks decreased between 1980 and 1993, from 3.6% to 3.5%.

Table 4 shows another interesting pattern. The proportionate representation of both White men and women in faculty ranks increases as they ascend the academic ladder from assistant professor to professor. In contrast, the proportionate representation of minority men and women in

TABLE 4

Faculty by Race, Ethnicity, Academic Rank, and Sex, 1981 and 1993

Academic Rank	White		Black		Latino		Asian		American Indian	
	1981	1993	1981	1993	1981	1993	1981	1993	1981	1993
Men										
All Ranks	88.2%	88.5%	3.7%	3.8%	2.1%	2.1%	5.8%	5.3%	.2%	.3%
Professor	99.8%	91.3%	2.1%	2.3%	1.3%	1.4%	4.6%	4.8%	.2%	.2%
Assoc. Prof.	89.4%	88.9%	3.4%	3.7%	1.8%	1.9%	5.2%	5.3%	.2%	.2%
Asst. Prof.	83.5%	84.2%	5.1%	5.4%	2.5%	2.7%	8.6%	7.4%	.3%	.3%
Instructor	87.0%	85.6%	5.7%	6.2%	3.4%	3.6%	3.3%	3.4%	.6%	1.2%
Lecturer	85.5%	86.7%	6.1%	5.9%	3.4%	3.0%	4.2%	4.0%	.5%	.4%
Women										
All Ranks	86.6%	86.6%	6.9%	6.9%	2.5%	2.6%	3.6%	3.5%	.4%	.4%
Professor	89.6%	88.7%	5.2%	5.8%	1.8%	2.3%	3.1%	2.9%	.3%	.3%
Assoc. Prof.	88.4%	88.5%	6.3%	6.2%	1.9%	1.9%	3.2%	3.1%	.2%	.3%
Asst. Prof.	85.6%	85.3%	7.2%	7.3%	2.6%	2.7%	4.3%	4.3%	.3%	.4%
Instructor	85.9%	85.2%	7.8%	7.9%	3.0%	3.2%	2.8%	3.0%	.5%	.7%
Lecturer	84.6%	85.0%	7.0%	6.8%	3.6%	3.4%	4.4%	4.4%	.4%	.4%

Source: National Center for Education Statistics, 1986, 1996.

faculty ranks increases as they descend the academic ladder from professor to assistant professor. Moreover, relative to other minority men, Asian men account for the largest proportion at the ranks of professor, associate professor, and assistant professor. In contrast, relative to other minority women, Black women account for the largest proportion at the ranks of professor, associate professor, and assistant professor. The proportionate representation of minority men and women in the faculty ranks remains overshadowed by the disproportionate representation of White men and women in the faculty ranks, however.

Doctoral Degrees and Faculty Representation

The number of doctoral degrees awarded in 1980 and 1993 by recipients' race, ethnicity, and sex is presented in Table 5. The number of doctoral degrees awarded to men between 1980 and 1993 decreased by 7.2% but increased 45.2% for

TABLE 5

Doctoral Degrees by Sex, Race, and Ethnicity, 1980 and 1993

Population	1980		1993		Change 1980–1993
	N	*%*	*N*	*%*	
Total	28,636	100.0	31,611	100.0	10.4%
Men	19,031	66.5	17,661	55.9	−7.2%
Women	9,605	33.5	13,950	44.1	45.2%
White	25,908	100.0	27,156	100.0	4.8%
Men	17,310	66.8	15,126	55.7	−12.6%
Women	8,598	33.2	12,030	44.3	39.9%
Black	1,265	100.0	1,393	100.0	10.1%
Men	694	54.9	631	45.3	−9.1%
Women	571	45.1	762	54.7	33.5%
Latino	456	100.0	903	100.0	98.0%
Men	277	60.7	465	51.5	67.9%
Women	197	39.3	438	48.5	144.7%
Asian	877	100.0	2,025	100.0	130.9%
Men	655	74.7	1,373	67.8	109.6%
Women	222	25.3	652	32.2	193.7%
Am. Ind.	130	100.0	134	100.0	3.1%
Men	95	73.1	66	49.3	−30.5%
Women	35	26.9	68	50.7	94.3%

Source: National Center for Education Statistics, 1986, 1996.

women. For purposes of discussion, let us assume that doctoral degree recipients are a primary recruiting pool for faculty positions. That is, recipients of doctoral degrees have a high degree of probability of seeking a faculty position. Although no one-to-one correlation exists between receiving a doctoral degree and pursuing a faculty position, one can assume with a high degree of confidence that doctoral degree recipients are highly visible in the faculty population.

Table 5 shows that although the number of doctoral degrees awarded to men decreased 7.2% between 1980 and 1993, the number of men in the faculty population increased 5.1% during the same time (Table 1). In comparison, the number of doctoral degrees awarded to women between 1980 and 1993 increased 45.2%, while their number in the faculty population increased 53.5%. If doctoral degrees are a primary vehicle for gaining access to the faculty ranks, then women appear to have made appreciable gains between 1980 and 1993. Men also made gains in the faculty ranks despite a reduction in the number receiving doctoral degrees between 1980 and 1993.

An examination of the relative differences among groups in Table 5 shows that although the number of White and Black males earning doctoral degrees between 1980 and 1993 decreased by 12.6% and 9.1%, respectively, the number of White and Black males in the faculty population increased 1.6% and 18.2%, respectively (Table 1). In comparison, the number of White and Black women earning doctoral degrees between 1980 and 1993 increased by 39.9% and 33.5%, respectively, while their number in the faculty population increased by 50.5% and 33.3%, respectively. The number of American Indian men earning doctoral degrees decreased by 30.5%, while their number in the faculty population increased 25% between 1980 and 1993. In contrast, the number of American Indian women earning doctoral degrees increased by 94.3%, while their number in the faculty population increased 60%.

The number of Latino men earning doctoral degrees between 1980 and 1993 increased 67.9%, while their number in the faculty population increased 40%. The number of Latino women earning doctoral degrees increased 144.7%, their number in the faculty population increased 150%. The number of Asian men earning doctoral degrees increased 109.6% and their number in

the faculty population increased 72.7% between 1980 and 1993. The number of Asian women earning doctoral degrees increased 193.7% and their number in the faculty population increased 200% during the same time.

An examination of the association between the number of doctoral degrees awarded and the number of persons in the faculty population between 1980 and 1993 shows that the association is close for Black women, Latinas, and Asian women. That is, increases in the number of doctoral degrees awarded correspond with numerical increases in the faculty population. For example, the number of Black women who earned doctoral degrees between 1980 and 1993 increased 33.5%, while their number in the faculty population increased 33.3%. In comparison, the number of Latino women and Asian women earning doctoral degrees increased 144.7% and 193.7%, respectively, while their number in the faculty population increased 150% and 200%, respectively. The increase in the number of White women earning doctoral degrees between 1980 and 1993 was appreciatively lower (39.9%) than the increase in their number in the faculty population (50.5%). In contrast, the increase in the number of American Indian women earning doctoral degrees was appreciatively larger (94.3%) than the increase in their number in the faculty population (60%).

Among men, the number earning doctoral degrees between 1980 and 1993 increased only for Latinos and Asians, 67.9% and 109.6%, respectively. The increase was noticeably larger than the increase in their number in the faculty population, however, 40% and 72.7%, respectively. In contrast, the number of White men, Black men, and American Indian men earning doctoral degrees between 1980 and 1993 decreased by 12.6%, 9.1%, and 30.5%, respectively, while the increase in their numbers in the faculty population was noticeable—1.6%, 18.2%, and 25%, respectively.

A caveat is necessary about the data in Table 5. The data show that minorities made gains in the number of doctoral degrees received between 1980 and 1993, but one must be careful not to interpret the data to show that the minority population in the United States is making appreciable gains in its postsecondary educational pursuits. For example, it is not possible to determine the nativity status of doctoral recipients in the minority population: Consider that the noticeable increases in the number of doctoral degrees

One must be careful not to interpret the data to show that the minority population in the United States is making gains in its postsecondary educational pursuits.

awarded to Latinos (98%) and Asians (131%) may not necessarily be associated with U.S. Latinos or Asians. According to Magner (1997), although the number of minority Ph.D.'s has been rising, "the proportion of those awarded to U.S. citizens who are black, Hispanic, Asian, or American Indian was unchanged, at about 13 percent" (p. A10). If foreign students are enumerated in statistics regarding the minority population and their number is increasing more than the number of persons in the minority population that are U.S. citizens, then the number of doctoral degrees awarded to persons in the minority population must be viewed with caution. Although minorities who are U.S. citizens are making gains in their educational pursuits, especially in the awarding of doctoral degrees, their gains may also include those of persons who are foreign students.

A Matter of Representativeness
The research literature on women faculty shows that although women have made gains in their numerical representation within the faculty population, the gains have not mirrored the numerical representation of women in U.S. society (Bentley and Blackburn, 1992; Chused, 1988; Everett, DeLoach, and Bressan, 1996; Simeone, 1987; Sowers-Hoag and Harrison, 1991). According to Table 1, for example, women accounted for 33.6% and men 66.4% of the faculty population in 1993. In contrast, women accounted for 51.3% and men 48.7% of the U.S. population (Aguirre and Turner, 1998). Based on their representation in U.S. society, women would appear to be underrepresented and men overrepresented in the faculty population. The contrast becomes more alarming when one considers that there are twice as many men in the faculty population as there are women. Although affirmative action was not designed to achieve parity between men and women, it has had "little impact on higher education. Women . . . still aren't present in the faculty in significant numbers" (Cadet, 1989, p. 16). Similarly, "after more than 15 years of affirmative action efforts aimed at recruiting and hiring women and minority faculty members, the number of women in tenured and tenure-track positions is still disappointingly low" (Rausch, Ortiz, Douthitt, and Reed, 1989, p. 1).

The research literature on women faculty also shows that the entry of women into the faculty ranks has lagged behind the number of women that have earned doctoral degrees (Hewlett, 1986; Simeone, 1987). Bogart (1985) has observed that "as impressive as are the increases in the number of women earning degrees in male-dominated occupational fields . . . women continue to experience restricted access to employment and promotion" (p. 471). "Although women make up more than half of U.S. undergraduates and are earning one-third of all doctorates, they hold only 12 percent of tenured faculty positions" (Cadet, 1989, p. 16). Similarly, "on the positive side, the record is clear that both the number and the percentage of women earning doctorates in all fields has been increasing since 1965. . . . On the negative side, one reads that women are concentrated in the lower professorial ranks . . . and have lower salaries even when occupying the same rank as their male counterparts" (Bentley and Blackburn, 1992, p. 697). The Committee on the Status of Women in the Economics Profession reports that women earning Ph.D. degrees in economics are more likely to find jobs in non-Ph.D.-granting departments located in small private or state institutions (Bartlett, 1997).

Are women earning doctorates in greater numbers than their entry into the faculty ranks? Although comparisons are not always free of intervening influences, such as competing methods for gathering the data, an examination of Tables 1 and 5 can help to answer the question. According to Table 5, the number of women earning doctoral degrees increased 45.2% between 1980 and 1993, with women earning 44% of the doctoral degrees awarded in 1993. In comparison, the number of men earning doctoral degrees between 1980 and 1993 decreased by 7.2%. According to Table 1, the number of women in the faculty population increased 53.5% between 1980 and 1993, with women making up 34% of the faculty population in 1993. In contrast, the number of men in the faculty population increased 5.1% between 1980 and 1993. Even if the data contain possible methodological limitations, it appears that the increase of women in the faculty population between 1980 and 1993 was slightly greater than the increase of women earning doctoral degrees. The increase of men in the faculty population was also noticeably greater than the increase in the number of men earning doctoral degrees. The proportionate representation of women in the faculty population for 1980 and 1993, 25.8% and 33.6%, respectively, however, was lower than their proportionate representation in the population of persons receiving doctoral degrees. In comparison, the proportionate representation of men in the faculty population in 1980 and 1993, 74.2% and 66.4%, respectively, was greater than the proportionate representation of men earning doctoral degrees, 66.5% and 55.9%, respectively.

Although women appear to have made gains in their representation in the faculty population and in the number of women earning doctoral degrees, their gains in the faculty population have been concentrated in the lower rungs of the academic ladder (Riger and others, 1997; Finkel and Olswang, 1994). Table 6, for example, presents the distribution of men and women in the faculty population by academic rank. According to the table, the distribution of men at all academic ranks decreased between 1980 and 1993, while the distribution of women increased during the same time. Moreover, the change in the distribution of women in the faculty population between 1980 and 1993 becomes noticeable as one descends the academic ladder. In contrast, the change in the distribution of men in the faculty population becomes noticeable as one ascends the academic ladder. And differences in the distribution of men and women faculty are less noticeable at the non-tenure-earning ranks of instructor and lecturer. In sum, despite the gains made by women in the faculty ranks, men continue to occupy the majority of the faculty ranks.

Although women appear to have made gains in their representation in the faculty population and in the number of women earning doctoral degrees, their gains in the faculty population have been concentrated in the lower rungs of the academic ladder.

TABLE 6

Men and Women Faculty by Academic Rank, 1980 and 1993

Academic Rank	Men		Women	
	1980	*1993*	*1980*	*1993*
All Ranks	73.3%	66.4%	26.7%	33.6%
Professor	89.7%	83.1%	10.3%	16.9%
Associate Professor	79.2%	69.9%	20.8%	30.1%
Assistant Professor	66.4%	57.1%	33.6%	42.9%
Instructor	57.3%	50.5%	42.7%	49.5%
Lecturer	57.1%	48.5%	42.9%	51.5%

Source: National Center for Education Statistics, 1996.

Minority Faculty

The data in this section show that the numerical representation of minority persons in the faculty population grew between 1980 and 1993. Between 1980 and 1993, for instance, Black persons increased their representation in the faculty population by 25%, Latinos by 71.4%, Asians by 92.3%, and American Indians by 38.5% (Table 1). As shown in Table 1, the proportionate representation of Blacks in the faculty population in 1993 was 4.7%, for Latinos 2.3%, for Asians 4.7%, and for American Indians 0.3%. In contrast, Blacks accounted for 12%, Latinos 8.8%, Asians 2.9%, and American Indians 0.8% of the U.S. population (Aguirre and Turner, 1998). Blacks, Latinos, and American Indians are underrepresented in the faculty population given their representation in the U.S. population. Asians, however, are overrepresented in the faculty population given their representation in the U.S. population.

Some of the research literature regarding the educational gains of the Asian population argues that the gains often result in the misconception that Asians do not face discriminatory practices (Chew, 1996; Moy, 1995; Nakanishi, 1988; Takagi, 1994). In particular, the noticeable presence of Asian faculty relative to other minority populations is often interpreted to show that discriminatory or unfair employment practices are missing in academia (Nakanishi, 1993). The perception that Asians are making more gains in the faculty ranks than other minority groups has also resulted in the misconception that they do not need support from programs such as affirmative action that address issues of equity and discrimination (Sands, Parson, and Duane, 1992; Yen, 1996). As a result, misconceptions about "how well" Asian faculty are doing in academia may hide discriminatory practices they face.

Minority persons increased their representation in the population of persons receiving doctoral degrees between 1980 and 1993—10.1% for Blacks, 98% for Latinos, 130.9% for Asians, and 3.1% for American Indians. The data in Table 5 also show that minority persons accounted for 9.5% of the doctoral degrees awarded in 1980 and 14.1% of the doctoral degrees awarded in 1993. The total number of doctoral degrees awarded to minority persons increased by 63.3% between 1980 and 1993.

The number of minority faculty increased 54.5% between 1980 and 1993 (see Table 1). According to the data in Table 7, the representation of minority persons in the faculty ranks increased 3.1 percentage points between 1980 and 1993, from 9.1% to 12.2%. The increase in the number of minority persons earning doctoral degrees between 1980 and 1993 (63.3%) was higher than the increase in their number in the faculty ranks between 1980 and 1993 (54.5%). Interestingly, the representation of minority persons in the population of persons earning doctoral degrees in 1980 (9.5%) was similar to their representation in the faculty ranks (9.1%). In 1993, however, minority persons accounted for 14.1% of the doctoral degrees awarded and 12.2% of the faculty population. Similar to the distribution of women faculty in the faculty ranks, the *representativeness* of minority persons becomes more noticeable as one descends the rungs in the academic ladder. As such, women and minorities become more visible in the faculty population as one descends the academic ranks.

Summary

The statistical data reviewed in this section show several pertinent conclusions. First, regardless of race and

TABLE 7

Minority Faculty Population by Sex, and Academic Rank, 1980 and 1993

| | *Minority Faculty** | | | | | |
| | *Total* | | *Men* | | *Women* | |
Academic Rank	*1980*	*1993*	*1980*	*1993*	*1980*	*1993*
All Ranks	9.1%	12.2%	6.0%	7.7%	3.1%	4.5%
Professor	6.6%	9.1%	5.6%	7.2%	1.0%	1.9%
Associate Professor	8.1%	11.2%	5.9%	7.8%	2.2%	3.4%
Assistant Professor	10.7%	15.3%	6.8%	9.0%	3.9%	6.3%
Instructor	10.8%	14.4%	5.7%	7.2%	5.1%	7.2%
Lecturer	10.7%	14.4%	5.9%	6.8%	4.8%	7.6%

*Minority faculty in the U.S. faculty population.

Source: National Center for Education Statistics, 1996.

ethnicity, the number of women in the faculty population increased more than the number of men between 1980 and 1993. Second, of the four minority groups, the number of Asians showed the largest increase in the number of faculty. Third, an examination of the association between the number of doctoral degrees awarded and the number of people in the faculty population between 1980 and 1993 shows that (a) the number of Black women, Latinas, and Asian women in the faculty population increased compared with the number earning doctoral degrees; (b) the numerical increase of White women in the faculty population was greater than the increase in the number earning doctoral degrees; (c) the numerical increase of American Indian women earning doctoral degrees was greater then their numerical increase in the faculty population; (d) only Latino men and Asian men showed an increase in the number earning doctoral degrees, but the increase was also greater than their numerical increase in the faculty population; and (e) although White men, Black men, and American Indian men showed decreases in the number earning doctoral degrees, they had noticeable numerical increases in the faculty population. Finally, the *representativeness* of women and minorities in the faculty population becomes noticeable as one descends the rungs of the academic ladder.

THE ACADEMIC WORKPLACE

The popular image of academia is of an *ivory tower,* a place shielded by ivy-covered walls from the demands of a world outside. In the ivory tower, scholars bask in enlightened discourse. Derrick Bell (1986) portrays academia as Camelot, a castle "located high on an impressive mountain, so high that it is often invisible in the mists and clouds that abound at such altitudes" (p. 385). The people inside the castle refer to themselves as *academicians* who "maintain whenever asked, and sometimes even when no one inquires, that their dedication is to the *Life of the Mind.* Absolutely no one knows what that means" (p. 386). Life in academia is seen as distant from everyday life.

Images of academia in popular literature focus on institutional features that set it apart from everyday life. Randall Jarrell (1952) describes life in Benton, a fictional women's college, as serene: "Benton was, all in all, a surprisingly contented place. . . . The ranks of the teachers of Benton were fairly anomalous. . . . Their salaries were fairly similar, and most of what power there was was distributed; being the head of a department, even, was a rotated chore. What mattered at Benton was the Approval of Your Colleagues, the respect of the community of Benton" (p. 94). Similarly, Mary McCarthy (1951) describes Jocelyn, a fictional college, as a peaceful place for faculty: "For the faculty . . . Jocelyn was by and large lotus-land. . . . The headship of departments [was] nominal, falling, by common consent, to the member with the greatest taste for paper-work" (p. 82).

Is academia really such a peaceful institution? Thomas Scheff (1995) describes life in academia as organized by activities similar to those found in street gangs.

> *Just as members of street gangs earn most of their livelihood from theft, academics gain most of theirs from careers. Being a member in good standing of a gang and a supergang is crucially important for advancement of one's career. There is little chance of advancement in the academy without hard work, but flaunting membership in gang and clan can certainly supplement or even substitute for talent and intelligence. Clearly and repeatedly showing one's loyalty to these groups can be most helpful in obtaining research grants and acceptance of publications, twin lifebloods of the academic career.* (pp. 157–158)

In a fictional account of status and prestige among faculty at an Ivy League school, Marshall Jevons (1985) notes:

There was a social hierarchy that defined one's caste in the Ivy League. The untenured were the untouchables of a university's caste system. And while not as severe as untouchability in India, a breakdown of this social organization would require a figure of no less than Gandhian proportions. (p. 19)

Scheff's and Jevons's descriptions of academia suggest that conflict and unequal relations are features of academic life. These features may be missing in popular thinking about academia because they are visible only to those inside academia and those most likely to be affected by them. They may also be missing in popular thinking because academia limits access to persons most likely to protect it from the outside world. Not only are they academicians, in Derrick Bell's view, they are also academia's most loyal protectors. The academicians can have meaning to themselves only if they promote an image of academia as comfortable and peaceful.

This section identifies and describes select features of the academic workplace, using several questions to guide the discussion: Are there competing images of academia in the research literature? What features socialize persons in the academic workplace? How does the academic culture affect identification with the workplace? What role does gender play in determining perceptions of the workplace?

Images of Academe

According to Page Smith (1990), the modern university has compromised its body by living "off the federal grants and corporate contracts while engaging in the most sordid and immoral practices *re* big-time sports" (p. 17). One result is that academia is populated by "atomized individuals known as specialists who hardly talk to each other, let alone to their colleagues in other fields" (p. 17). According to Scheff (1995), the search for specialized knowledge by faculty depends on "ignoring other clans and gangs" in academia as a "risk-free way of maintaining unitary groups" (p. 161).

Smith also argues that academia's use of *research* to attract funding from government agencies and corporations compromises the integrity of academia. Academia's ability to "tap into government largesse has played a major role in determining the composition and character of university faculties. Many professors have been appointed to important chairs primarily because they had reputations for attracting large government grants" (Smith, 1990, pp. 11–12). In 1994, Hahnemann University threatened to dismiss faculty who did not generate at least 50% of their salary from research grants (Mangan, 1994). The pressure on faculty to generate research funding has increased their disenchantment with academic work (Plater, 1995). Academia's focus on research thus plays an important role in defining the objectives of academic work and the character of the faculty.

In contrast to Page Smith's view of academia, George Keller (1983) describes academia as an institutional entity that competes with organizations in society, not just educational ones, for valued resources and political influence:

American colleges and universities occupy a special, hazardous zone in society, between the competitive profit-making business sector and the government owned and run state agencies. They are dependent yet free; market-oriented yet outside cultural and intellectual fashions. The faculty are inventors, entrepreneurs, and retailers of knowledge, aesthetics, and sensibility yet professional like the clergy or physicians. The institutions pay no taxes but are crucial to economic development. They conduct their business much as their European counterparts did in the Renaissance, still proud and pedantic as Rabelais saw those forerunners; yet modern corporations pay them to sniff out the future. (p. 5)

Keller's characterization of academia focuses on its ability to compete and market itself in society. The faculty are not only teachers in Keller's characterization; they are also the architects of academia's ability to survive in a competitive marketplace. As academia enters the 21st century, faculty will need to assume greater responsibility for its survival by becoming more efficient in the use of institutional resources, such as research grants, to meet market uncertainties, such as decreasing student enrollment (Kerr, 1997).

Tierney and Bensimon (1996) suggest that there are two competing images of academia, a *conservative image* and a *liberal humanist image.* The conservative image characterizes faculty as "largely ideological and radical . . . disengaged intellectuals who prefer to conduct esoteric research rather than teach undergraduate courses. . . . Faculty are parodied as misanthropes who want to be left alone to develop obscure theories that are ideologically tainted" (pp. 7–8). On the other hand, the liberal humanist view portrays the university as "devoted to the life of the mind. The triple functions of the university—research, teaching, and service—are still important. . . . Scholars need distance from the everyday world in order to deal with intellectual issues, yet it is their responsibility to provide creative ideas for dealing with social and environmental problems" (p. 10). Which image, conservative or liberal humanist, one identifies with will depend on one's ideological beliefs. If one believes that academia is a vehicle for faculty to alter values in society, then one will adopt a conservative view of higher education (see Kimball, 1990; Bloom, 1987). In comparison, if one believes that academia is a means for introducing ideas into society that result in constructive social change, then one will adopt a humanistic view of higher education (see Smith, 1990).

The preceding images illustrate the range and difference of activity in academia. Although the images may appear to contradict each other, together they create a portrait of academia. First, academia is a complex institution that uses its resources, especially research and faculty, to compete with other organizations in society. Second, the strategies academia uses to compete with other organizations determine the type and level of competition between faculty and academic departments. One outcome of the competition for faculty and academic departments is that academic power is not shared equally inside academia. Third, nested within academia's institutional environment are vehicles—research, teaching, and service—that allow faculty to pursue independence and autonomy in their work roles. Although the faculty's independence and autonomy may be viewed as a threat to values and order in society, they are vital for infusing ideas into society that promote positive and constructive social change.

Academic Culture

Do these images of academia suggest that there is an *academic culture?* If an academic culture does exist, what are its principal features? For the purposes of discussion, *culture* is defined as "the collective programming of the mind [that] distinguishes the members of one human group from another; the interactive aggregate of common characteristics that influences a human group's response to its environment" (Hofstede, 1980, p. 25). Culture is able to provide persons with a collective identity because it provides them with a "set of values that leads to individual preferences and a system of technical knowledge that informs individuals about which means to choose in order to achieve specified ends" (Meyer, Boli, and Thomas, 1994, p. 12). Culture thus socializes persons to a common worldview, perceptions of the environment, and value orientation. For example, academic life is a *lifestyle* that socializes faculty to perform and to value activities that are vital to membership in the academic community, such as attending professional meetings with other faculty involved in "giving papers, organizing panels, perhaps participating on editorial boards and writing book reviews" (Stewart, 1995, p. 335). As a result, faculty are identified as participants in the academic culture. For further discussion about the academic culture, see Clark, 1972; Dill, 1982; Kuh and Whitt, 1988; Tierney, 1988.

If their participation in activities gives faculty a sense of identity with an academic culture, then identification of the activities can instruct us about the academic culture. In particular, the perceptions held by faculty about professional goals may tell us how they perceive an academic culture. Implicit in our discussion are the assumptions that academic culture provides codes for organizing faculty behavior. We also assume that how faculty behave in academia is a response to those codes. As a result, how faculty identify their professional goals will instruct us about the institutional expectations for the goals, namely the academic culture.

According to Table 8, *being a good teacher* and *being a good colleague* are important goals for faculty. The high level of support expressed by faculty for the two goals suggests that they are principal features of what may be referred to as *an academic worldview*. The level of support for the goals also reinforces the general perception that academia is free of intergroup conflict. That is, "to be a good

TABLE 8

Professional Goals of Full-Time Faculty by Sex, 1989–1990 and 1995–1996

Professional Goal	1989–1990[1]			1995–1996[2]		
	Total	Men	Women	Total	Men	Women
Be a good teacher	98.2%	98.1%	98.4%	99.2%	99.1%	99.3%
Be a good colleague	80.0%	77.4%	86.4%	86.6%	84.5%	90.9%
Engage in research	58.5%	61.1%	52.3%	54.6%	57.5%	48.7%
Engage in outside activities	52.5%	49.8%	59.1%	49.3%	45.8%	56.3%
Provide services to the community	43.4%	39.9%	52.0%	41.9%	37.6%	50.3%
Participate in committee or other administrative work	29.2%	25.7%	37.9%	28.3%	24.2%	36.6%

[1]Special tabulation, "The American College Teacher: National Norms for the 1989–90 H.E.R.I. Faculty Survey," UCLA Higher Education Research Institute.

[2]Special tabulation, "The American College Teacher: National Norms for the 1995–96 H.E.R.I. Faculty Survey," UCLA Higher Education Research Institute.

teacher" and "to be a good colleague" promote an image of academia in which faculty participate in a harmonious context that links organizational goals (being a good teacher) with personal goals (being a good colleague). In this context, faculty also provide each other with an "understanding of the purpose or meaning of their organization and their work" (Peterson and Spencer, 1990, p. 4). Not only does the context socialize faculty to a shared social identity, it also uses the social identity to instruct faculty about how academia differs from other institutional settings. In particular, the belief is promoted among faculty members that they are a *community of scholars* that collectively governs academia (Mortimer and McConnell, 1978; Chaffee and Tierney, 1988; Clark, 1970).

According to Rice (1986), research is "the central professional endeavor and the focus of academic life" (p. 14). Given its centrality to academic activity, it is not surprising to find that research promotes hierarchical relationships in academia (Bell, 1966; Jencks and Riesman, 1968; Clark, 1985). That is, research has resulted in a hierarchical arrangement of higher education institutions in which the *research university* is the top of the hierarchy. For example, the Carnegie classifications for institutions of higher education include Research Universities I, Research Universities II, Doctoral Universities I, and Doctoral Universities II. The difference between Type I and Type II research universities is based on the amount of federal support, especially grants, each receives. Type I institutions are generally regarded as the target population for institutions interested in raising their academic status.

Table 8 also notes that *engaging in research* is a professional goal pursued by most faculty. Interestingly, the pursuit of this goal decreased in faculty support between 1989–90 and 1995–96. In contrast, being a good teacher and being a good colleague are goals that increased in support among faculty between 1989–90 and 1995–96. The decrease in support for engaging in research does not necessarily indicate that faculty have lost interest in conducting research. Rather, the decrease in support may reflect changes that have taken place in the research marketplace, especially the availability of research funds. For example, reductions by Congress in the allocation of research monies to funding agencies, such as the National Endowment for the Humanities, National Science Foundation, and National Institute of Mental Health, have increased the competition among faculty for fewer research dollars (Hanson, 1995; Macilwain, 1997; Lawler, 1995). One outcome is that although faculty still support engaging in research as a professional goal, they may have increased their support of other professional goals to compensate for decreasing research funding (Plater, 1995). And the decreased research funding may have resulted in faculty's focusing more on "quality of life" in academia, such as being a good teacher and being a good colleague.

Second, consider that during the last decade academia has come under attack for neglecting teaching and promoting research as a tool for obtaining economic resources and for using the curriculum to alter basic American values (Kimball, 1990; Bloom, 1987; D'Souza, 1991; Sykes, 1988). It would then not be surprising to find that the limited availability of research funding has promoted greater faculty interest in other institutional activities—especially teaching and collegiality (Austin and Gamson, 1983). Thus, the support among faculty for research, teaching, and collegiality shows "the belief that university and colleges are involved in 'good work,' that is, the production of knowledge for society and the intellectual development of students and . . . a commitment to collegiality coupled with autonomy as the appropriate organizational context within which faculty should work" (Austin, 1990, p. 65).

Table 8 also notes that faculty support for the goals of *engaging in outside activities* and *providing services to the community* decreased between 1989–90 and 1995–96. Because *consultation* is a principal reason for faculty involvement in outside activities, the limited availability of research funds may have also resulted in fewer dollars to pay consultants for their expertise. As a result, decreased support among the faculty for engaging in outside activities may simply reflect marketplace conditions for consultants and their services.

Similarly, the decrease in faculty support for providing services to the community may reflect changes in how academia responds to the community (Rickard, 1993; Roberts, 1993; Schomberg and Farmer, 1994). For example, the response to community needs, such as providing a place for reentering students, preparing high school students for college, and linking educational goals with occupational opportunities, has prompted academia to create organizational units to address such community needs. That is, the degree of organizational specialization has increased regarding community services. Consequently, the recruitment of personnel for these specialized organizational units has reduced the faculty's role in responding to community needs. From another perspective, increased organizational specialization allows academia to compete with other postsecondary organizations for foundation and government money that targets community needs.

Finally, Table 8 also shows that faculty support is not strong regarding participation in committee or other administrative work. On the one hand, faculty may regard participation in committee or administrative work as not complementing or extrinsic to the goals of teaching, research, and collegiality (Peterson and White, 1992). On the other hand, faculty may regard participation in committee or administrative work as *busy work* that is not vital to organizational decision making. Thus, faculty may regard participation in committee or administrative work as a constraint on their autonomy, especially if one considers that participation requires that faculty comply, and monitor their colleagues' compliance, with organizational expectations (Austin and Gamson, 1983; Blackburn and Lawrence, 1995).

The Relationship Between Academic Culture and the Academic Workplace

Another strategy to use in examining the academic culture is to examine faculty perceptions of factors that identify the academic workplace. Implicit in this strategy is the assumption that faculty responses to features of the workplace provide information regarding the institutional dimensions that define the workplace for faculty. Faculty responses to workplace features also provide information about how faculty conceptualize the academic workplace (Clark, 1984; Feild and Giles, 1977). The observations one is able to make from an examination of the perceptions held by faculty about the workplace can help us understand the faculty's interpretation of "how organizational life actually does function and how it should function. These perceptions may be accurate or inaccurate, but they represent reality from the perspective of participants" (Peterson and Spencer, 1990, p. 12). Thus, faculty perceptions of the workplace identify the *climate* in the academic workplace for faculty (Allaire and Firsirotu, 1984; Peterson, Cameron, Jones, Meta, and Ettington, 1986).

Table 9 lists faculty responses to certain characteristics of the workplace. There are few differences in how men and women respond to such characteristics. According to the table, the characteristic of the workplace that faculty are most satisfied with has to do with *autonomy and independence.* The research literature notes that faculty express greater satisfaction with "intrinsic" factors in the workplace such as autonomy and independence than with "extrinsic" factors such as salary and administrative work (Hill, 1986–87; Kanter, 1980; Pearson and Seiler, 1983; Smith, Anderson, and Lovrich, 1995). Since one of the expectations of faculty in academia is for them to be creative thinkers and innovative teachers, then it is appropriate for academia to create a workplace climate that uses autonomy and independence to promote faculty members' intellectual pursuits.

The characteristic of the workplace that faculty are most satisfied with has to do with autonomy and independence.

Table 9 indicates that faculty are satisfied with faculty relationships in the workplace. Recall that in Table 8 "being a good colleague" is an important professional goal for faculty. If we couple these observations, then we can suggest that faculty satisfaction in the workplace is an indicator of how the academic culture facilitates the attainment of professional goals: "Educational institutions advance not just with faculty participation but usually under faculty initiative" (Stewart, 1995, p. 339). From an institutional perspective, the academic culture promotes a workplace climate that weaves professional goals with institutional expectations.

Not surprisingly, according to Table 9, faculty are satisfied with their teaching assignments. Table 8 also indicates that being a good teacher is an important professional goal for faculty. Together, these observations suggest that the academic culture creates a workplace climate that promotes the perception among faculty that teaching is important. Since one of the principal functions of academia is to teach students, then one would expect *teaching* to be an important institutional activity. And one would also expect faculty to perceive teaching as an important institutional activity, especially one that is central to the personnel review process (Rich and Jolicoeur, 1978). It is thus important that faculty,

TABLE 9

Faculty Satisfaction with the Workplace by Sex, 1989–1990 and 1995–1996

Workplace Characteristics	1989–1990[1]			1995–1996[2]		
	Total	Men	Women	Total	Men	Women
Autonomy and Independence	82.9%	83.3%	81.9%	86.2%	86.8%	85.0%
Relationships with other faculty	75.1%	74.5%	76.5%	76.8%	76.1%	78.0%
Teaching assignments	74.9%	75.8%	71.4%	81.0%	81.5%	79.5%
Relationship with administration	51.8%	50.7%	54.4%	56.1%	55.3%	57.6%
Opportunity for scholarly pursuits	45.4%	48.4%	37.8%	53.8%	57.3%	46.7%

[1]Special tabulation, "The American College Teacher: National Norms for the 1989–90 H.E.R.I. Faculty Survey," UCLA Higher Education Research Institute.
[2]Special tabulation, "The American College Teacher: National Norms for the 1995–96 H.E.R.I. Faculty Survey," UCLA Higher Education Research Institute.

as the primary agents in teaching, feel comfortable teaching and that they perceive the academic culture as valuing what they do as teachers. In the end, faculty want to teach and feel good about doing it: "We need to establish new rhythms, new ways of learning, new ways of celebrating. We need alternation and alternatives; action and response; freshening of the spirit and lightening of the mind. We need to teach" (Smith, 1990, p. 222).

Finally, according to Table 9, faculty are satisfied with their relationship with the administration and the opportunity for scholarly pursuits. If one considers the workplace characteristics of "relationship with administration" and "opportunity for scholarly pursuits" "extrinsic" workplace features, then it is not unexpected to find faculty expressing moderate levels of satisfaction with these characteristics of the workplace. That is, faculty may perceive these two workplace characteristics as associated with the work environment but not with the actual context for faculty work (Locke, Fitzpatrick, and White, 1983). For example, regarding the job satisfaction of college faculty, Hill (1986–87) has observed: "Things intrinsic to the work—teaching, scholarly achievement/creativity, the nature of the work, etc.—should be the principal sources of job satisfaction; concomitantly, factors extrinsic to the actual work—salary, fringe benefits, administrative features . . .— should emerge as the principal contributions to job dissatisfaction" (p. 38). It is not so much that faculty are dissatisfied with the workplace features of "relationship with administration" and "opportunity for scholarly pursuits" as it is that faculty may not associate these workplace features with their personal satisfaction in the workplace.

Interestingly, the faculty's dissatisfaction with the workplace is often associated with extrinsic factors rather than intrinsic factors. Finkelstein (1978) has observed that faculty "tend to derive satisfaction from the nature of their work itself, while they tend to express dissatisfaction most often with extrinsic factors, such as salary [and] administrative leadership" (p. 221). Other workplace characteristics that faculty perceive as extrinsic factors and that they associate with low levels of satisfaction include administrative and/or organizational decision making (Cohen, 1974), inadequate institutional resources (Gmelch, Lovrich, and Wilke, 1984), insufficient income (Gmelch, Wilke, and Lovrich, 1986), ambiguity in work role expectations (Smith, Anderson, and Lovrich, 1995), and lack of consistency in criteria for performance evaluations (Pearson and Seiler, 1983; Copeland and Murray, 1996). Smith and others (1995) suggest that faculty dissatisfaction with the workplace has increased because the quality of life for faculty in academia has become more stressful as a result of changes in the contextual features of academia:

> *The impact of fiscal changes brought on by two conservative national administrations and two recessions in the 1980s has left state budgets profoundly constrained and most university campuses in similar straits. Faculty salaries have declined over the past twenty years in relation to private-sector incomes, faculty salaries have not kept pace with inflation over this time period, salary disparities across disciplines have grown, and salary compression across ranks has occurred—all helping to create serious morale problems in the academic workplace.* (p. 266)

Diversity in Academia and the Academic Workplace
Academia generally tries to stay away from controversy. The institutional culture is designed to enhance academia's intellectual features rather than debate controversial issues. The topic of *diversity in the workplace* is, as a result, pregnant with controversy and debate for academia. *Diversity* in academia is driven by the belief that underrepresented populations, especially women and minorities, must be given access to academia (Levine, 1991). Although diversity initiatives in academia were initially focused on increasing *representation* of minority students, they have been expanded to cover all underrepresented groups. According to Hirano-Nakanishi (1994), "Representation, which began as an issue focused on students, now embraces staff, faculty, senior administrators, and trustees. Originally *representation* meant an increase from none to a few; today, representation means setting targets in proportion to societal populations. Originally, representation meant access for blacks; today it refers to access for any underrepresented group" (pp. 63–64).

Instead of becoming a vehicle for institutional change in academia, diversity initiatives have become a battleground.

Resistance to diversity initiatives is observed in the increasing social distance between non-White and White students on campus (Institute for the Study of Student Change, 1990; Buchen, 1992; Powell, 1998). Resistance to diversity initiatives by the faculty, especially White faculty, is observed in the obstacles women and minorities face in the academic workplace. Women and minority faculty, for example, are marginalized in the academic workplace with regard to their exclusion from institutional activities that govern academic life (Stassen, 1995; Gonzales, 1991; Chepyator-Thomson and King, 1996). In general, academia has resisted diversity initiatives despite the increasing multicultural character of U.S. society (Josey, 1993; Milem and Astin, 1993; Bromberg, 1993; Smart, 1978; Reed, 1986; Larwood, Gutek, and Gattiker, 1984).

Affirmative action is generally considered to be a remedial measure for increasing diversity in the academic workplace (McCombs, 1989; Brooks, 1982; Valverde, 1998). Perhaps the most noticeable aspect of affirmative action in the academic workplace is the controversy it attracts rather than its ability to radically increase diversity in the workplace. For example, the passage of Proposition 209 (anti—affirmative action) in California signaled the end of affirmative action in California society, especially in education (Aguirre, 1997). Proposition 209's passage increased rather than reduced questions regarding the *legitimacy* of minority students and faculty in academia (Bell, 1997a, 1997b). One result of Proposition 209's passage may be damage to the collegial relationships between White and minority faculty in the workplace (Malveaux, 1996). Another result of the proposition's passage may be a relaxed commitment to increasing the representation of minority faculty in California higher education (Schneider, 1998).

Regarding the effectiveness of affirmative action to diversity in the academic workplace, Tack and Patitu (1992) observe that "even though nearly two decades have passed since the enactment of affirmative action laws in the United States, higher education remains largely a white male enterprise" (p. 75). Despite decreasing numbers in the professoriat, from 68% in 1980 to 59% in 1993, White males occupy the majority of faculty positions (National Center for Education Statistics, 1986, 1996). The dominant position of White males in the U.S. professoriat reflects an ideology in academia that "despite its rhetoric, and its attention to the undeniable force of changing demographics, the power of tradition and past practice in higher education militate against the diversity it so desperately seeks" (Sanders and Mellow, 1990, p. 9). In other words, social forces may exist in the academic workplace that resist initiatives to increase diversity.

If one assumes that faculty are in a favorable position to observe how institutional decision making shapes academic culture, then faculty perceptions of how academic culture responds to diversity create a "picture of an institution's campus climate as experienced by the people who participate in the college or university community" (Edgert, 1994, p. 53). To this end, faculty responses to diversity initiatives are presented in Table 10. In general, according to the table, faculty perceive academia's response to increasing the representation of minorities in the faculty and administration as decreasing between 1989–90 and 1995–96 and academia's response to increasing the representation of women in the faculty and administration as increasing slightly. Interestingly, faculty perceive academia's response to creating a diverse multicultural environment on campus as increasing noticeably during the same time period.

The faculty's perception that academia has decreased its response to increasing the representation of minorities corresponds to an observation made by Bunzel (1990): "During the past two decades there has been an increase in the participation of under-represented minority groups on traditionally white faculties. However, despite the enactment of affirmative action plans by virtually every college and university, the rate of progress for minority faculty has decreased in recent years and has even regressed for black faculty" (pp. 43–44). That is, faculty may perceive academia as decreasing its response to increasing the representation of minorities despite the presence of an institutional vehicle, affirmative action, that supports and promotes efforts aimed at increasing institutional diversity. Although faculty perceive academia's response to increasing the representation of women as increasing, some researchers argue that academia's response falls short of reflecting the number of women earning doctoral degrees (Bentley and Blackburn, 1992; Billard, 1994).

Social forces may exist in the academic workplace that resist initiatives to increase diversity.

TABLE 10

Faculty Perceptions of Institutional Commitment to Diversity Issues by Sex, 1989–1990 and 1995–1996

Diversity Issue	1989–1990[1]			1995–1996[2]		
	Total	Men	Women	Total	Men	Women
Increase the representation of minorities in the faculty and administration	46.9%	46.1%	49.0%	45.0%	44.5%	46.0%
Increase the representation of women in the faculty and administration	39.2%	40.9%	34.8%	41.0%	44.5%	33.9%
Creating a diverse multicultural environment on campus	40.0%	38.2%	44.3%	50.3%	48.4%	54.0%

[1]Special tabulation, "The American College Teacher: National Norms for the 1989–90 H.E.R.I. Faculty Survey," UCLA Higher Education Research Institute.

[2]Special tabulation, "The American College Teacher: National Norms for the 1995–96 H.E.R.I. Faculty Survey," UCLA Higher Education Research Institute.

*Women are flocking to graduate schools in record
numbers, and many are specializing in fields that have
been traditionally dominated by men. . . . Decision
makers in many institutions of higher education may
pay lip service to affirmative action by developing
systems [that], on the surface, [seem] to seek and wel-
come women, but [that] really attempt to comply with
federal regulations on paper only. In reality, the number of women hired is still small, and of that number,
even fewer attain tenure and full professor status.*
(Granger, 1993, pp. 121, 123)

According to the data in Table 10, faculty perceive
academia as not having a noticeable change in its response
to increasing the number of women and minorities between
1989–90 and 1995–96. Why then do faculty perceive
academia as increasing diversity through a multicultural
environment on campuses during those same years?
Consider that the visibility of women and minorities on
campus may create the impression among faculty that
academia has been transformed into a *multicultural*
organization—especially if faculty notice women and
minorities participating in activities or occupying positions
from which they have been noticeably absent in the past.
As a result, faculty may perceive academia as a multicultural
organization "characterized by pluralism, full integration of
minority-culture members both formally and informally, an
absence of prejudice and discrimination, and low levels of
[intergroup] conflict" (Cox, 1991, pp. 46–47). It may be also
that faculty perceive academia as a race-neutral organization
and that changes in its environment, especially multiculturalism, are a reflection of academia's response to altering its
institutional character. Faculty may thus believe that
exclusion of minorities is no longer an institutional concern.
By focusing on issues of exclusion, faculty are omitting
minorities from their perceptions of academia through not
arguing for their inclusion (Nkomo, 1992). Or faculty may
just be complacent and believe that the "problem of closed
doors for minorities has been solved for all time" (Delgado,
1988, p. 409).

Finally, although both male and female faculty perceive
academia's response to increasing the representation of
minorities as decreasing between 1989–90 and 1995–96, only

women faculty perceive academia's response to increasing the representation of women as decreasing between 1989–90 and 1995–96. A noticeable difference exists in women faculty members' perceptions regarding the increased representation of women and minorities. That is, women faculty perceive academia as more responsive in increasing the representation of minorities than of women. In a sense, women faculty members' perception of academia's response to increasing the representation of women may reflect their belief that "hiring practices in higher education are changing, but even this reflects the ideology pervading the organization of all work in this country—that women's work, collectively and individually, is less valuable than men's" (Cadet, 1989, p. 17). Thus, while women faculty are more likely than men faculty to perceive academia as committed to creating a diverse multicultural environment, they may be less likely than men faculty to perceive academia as committed to increasing the representation of women. That is, women faculty may not perceive themselves as linked with academia's commitment to creating a diverse multicultural environment.

Summary

Academia is characterized in popular thinking as a paradise behind ivy-covered walls that shield academia from the world outside the walls and provide faculty with a sense of community. Despite the pastoral image of academia, the climate is one characterized by intense competition between faculty and academic departments over resources. And the competition over resources has resulted in a hierarchical arrangement that places research universities at the top.

Faculty perceive the academic workplace as promoting autonomy and independence. They also perceive autonomy and independence as necessary for satisfaction in the workplace. By linking personal goals with institutional expectations, faculty perceive the academic workplace as supportive of their professional socialization.

The increasing presence of social forces such as Proposition 209 and *Hopwood v. Texas* that argue against diversity make it necessary for us to examine academia's response to diversity. In general, faculty perceive academia as responding more to increasing the representation of women than of minorities in the faculty and administration. In addition, faculty perceive academia as having a noticeable response to creating a multicultural environment on campus, although women faculty are less likely than men faculty to perceive academia as responding to the need to increase the representation of women in the faculty and administration.

THE ACADEMIC WORKPLACE FOR WOMEN AND MINORITY FACULTY

The academic workplace has been described as *chilly* and *alienating* for women and minority faculty. Many of the obstacles faced by women and minority faculty in the academic workplace are the product of an institutional environment that serves the interests of White male faculty (Sandler and Hall, 1986; Washington and Harvey, 1989; Culp, 1992). According to McKay (1995), "The special problems that confront minority group faculty in mainstream white colleges and universities are rooted in the premises that informed Western culture's white, male-dominated, closed intellectual system for hundreds of years. . . . So closed, exclusive, and . . . elite was this system that for centuries it excluded everyone outside of its designated knowers, including Anglo-European women" (p. 50). Accordingly, Tack and Patitu (1992) observe, the institutional environment has remained typified by White male faculty despite academia's use of affirmative action rhetoric: "Even though nearly two decades have passed since the enactment of affirmative action laws in the United States, higher education remains largely a white male enterprise" (p. 75).

If the academic workplace serves the interests of White male faculty, then one would expect to find the presence of women and minority faculty constrained in the academic workplace (Henry and Nixon, 1994; Margolis and Romero, 1998; Sanders and Mellow, 1990). One would expect to find, for example, women and minority faculty occupying peripheral roles in the workplace. That is, gender and minority status would operate in the workplace as vehicles for placing women and minority faculty in peripheral roles. One result is that women and minority faculty are *marginalized* in the workplace by being overrepresented in *women* or *minority* activities. Thus, women and minority faculty are distanced from participating and competing in workplace activities with White male faculty (Aguirre, 1987; DiNitto, Aguilar, Franklin, and Jordan, 1995; Park, 1996).

Despite its portrayal as a community immune to the problems found in the world outside its ivy-covered walls, gender and minority status are used in academia in much the same way they are used in the world outside. According to Epps (1989), "the allocation of racial, ethnic, gender, and social-class groups within the academic hierarchy is consistent with the relative status, wealth, and power of these groups in American society" (p. 23). In other words, the status inequality associated with gender and minority status in the world outside is also found inside the ivy-covered walls of academia. Women and minority faculty are thus marginalized inside academia in much the same way they are marginalized as women and minority persons in the world outside.

Women and minority faculty are marginalized inside academia in much the same way they are marginalized as women and minority persons in the world outside.

This section examines and discusses the social forces that shape the institutional presence and participation of women and minority faculty in the academic workplace. The following questions serve as guides for the discussion: How do women and minority faculty perceive and define their participation in the academic workplace? What are the institutional factors that shape women's and minority faculty members' perceptions the workplace? What roles do women and minority faculty see themselves as performing in the academic workplace? What is the organizational fit of women and minority faculty in the academic workplace?

Issues in the Workplace for Women Faculty

An examination of faculty women's perceptions of the academic workplace found that women faculty perceive little opportunity to participate in decision making (Aguirre, Hernandez, and Martinez, 1994). The researchers found that women faculty perceive less opportunity to participate in institutional activities as they move from the departmental level to the college level. They found further that White women faculty perceive more opportunity to participate in institutional activities than minority women faculty. In general, the finding that women faculty perceive little opportunity to participate in decision-making activities corresponds with an observation that both White and minority women have not "achieved full access to the arenas that position them for leadership, or to leadership positions themselves" (Shavlik, Touchton, and Pearson, 1989, p. 447).

In a study of the academic experiences of women and men faculty, Rausch and others (1989) found that women faculty perceive less equity than men faculty in the allocation of responsibilities, such as teaching and committee assignments.

Eighty-one percent of the men felt that their amount of teaching responsibilities had almost always or always been equitable in relation to their colleagues while

*66 percent of the women felt the same way. And,
15 percent of the women felt that almost never or never
were teaching responsibilities distributed equally in
comparison to 8.8 percent of the men. Over 86 percent
of the men reported that they almost always or always
had an equitable share of committee responsibilities
but only 68.5 percent of the women had similar
perceptions.* (p. 7)

Accordingly, Wenzel and Hollenshead (1994) observed
that women faculty often leave a university position
because of the unequal opportunities they face
compared with men faculty. For example, women faculty
describe experiences in which men were offered more
institutional assistance with their careers, such as research
and laboratory money, than they were, citing them as
reasons for leaving.

Regarding the participation of women faculty in
institutional activities, the research literature notes that
women faculty are often assigned time-consuming tasks
that men faculty do not regard as important for professional
socialization (Chamberlain, 1988; Denton and Zeytinoglu,
1993; Parson, Sands, and Duane, 1991). Women faculty are
often the victims of negative portrayals in the academic
workplace that devalue their participation in workplace
activities (Gallant and Cross, 1993; Merritt and Reskin, 1992;
Henry, 1990). Women faculty perceive the workplace
environment as structuring workplace activities for men
faculty that enhance their professional socialization
(Ayer, 1984; Johnsrud and Des Jarlais, 1994; Hollon and
Gemmill, 1976). In general, the role played by women
faculty in the academic workplace is described as follows:

*Academic women have to learn to walk on eggshells,
playing two contradictory roles: the woman and the
professor. . . . They may be asked to pour the tea at a
faculty reception, to do the photocopying for the
department head whose secretary is away, to bake
cookies for a departmental gathering. They may be
asked for advice about sewing, interior decoration, and
gift-giving; if they're short, they may be called "our little
assistant professor" and even be patted on the head.*
(Toth, 1995, p. 40)

Although women faculty are relegated to peripheral activities in the academic workplace, the research literature also notes that women faculty experience a *gendered* workplace. That is, women faculty perceive the academic workplace as using gender as a status characteristic for allocating resources and opportunity. For example, compared with men, women faculty are assigned heavier teaching loads (Austin and Gamson, 1983) and more service responsibilities (Menges and Exum, 1983). Women faculty often find themselves excluded from participating in committees if their presence makes men faculty feel uncomfortable (Parson and others, 1991). Women faculty also believe that men faculty trivialize their research and publishing during academic review (Johnsrud and Wunsch, 1991). According to Steward and others (1995), the obstacles faced by women faculty in the academic workplace create a "climate within the academic work environment that can be personally and professionally toxic to many women who have attained faculty status" (p. 51).

Minority Women Faculty

According to the research literature, minority women faculty experience more barriers to their professional socialization in the workplace than White women faculty (Bernstein and Cock, 1994; Nieves-Squires, 1992; Wyche and Graves, 1992). The low number of minority women in faculty positions often becomes an obstacle for them in the academic workplace. For example, the lack of representation of Hispanic women faculty in academia causes them to be overly burdened by student affairs activities.

> *The lack of representation of Hispanas in academia as faculty members causes them to be overburdened by an inordinate amount of student advisees—both those who are formally assigned and those who gravitate toward their doors. . . . The sheer effort of trying to do well by the students while at the same time routing an academic career that encompasses scholarly research, excellent teaching, and committee participation ensures that very few Hispanas remain within the academic ranks.* (Nieves-Squires, 1992, p. 80)

Although minority women faculty are expected to perform similar activities as White women faculty, minority women faculty are also expected to perform *symbolic* roles in academia. "The professor of color is asked, and expected, to serve students of color as a *role model* and confidant. She is expected to be a special tutor and advisor to their student groups as well as a substitute mother/father/older sister/older brother figure" (Greene, 1991, p. 300). The symbolic roles minority women faculty are expected to perform in academia enhance their role incongruity. For example, according to a Japanese-American faculty woman:

> *I'm such a minority in this context or in any university context in this country pretty much. People like me have to adjust to the dominant system. . . . I don't like interacting in'that way. It's not a culturally preferred, culturally acceptable thing . . . and I resent that. But you don't hear a lot of us because there are not a lot of us saying we resent it. We always have to switch over into the other mode.* (quoted in Johnsrud and Sadao, 1998, p. 326)

In general, the obstacles faced by minority women faculty in academia are the product of two status characteristics, gender and minority status. On the one hand, they are expected to perform *gendered* roles in academia that require them to perform as caretakers for students—the big sister or mother role for minority students. On the other hand, minority women faculty are rendered powerless in academia by their minority status, and they are often regarded as tokens that satisfy two affirmative action slots (Wyche and Graves, 1992). In addition, the research literature shows that minority women faculty experience more discrimination in academia than their minority male counterparts (Montero-Sieburth, 1996; Singh, Robinson, and Williams-Green, 1995). "African American women in social work academe may be at a greater risk of experiencing discrimination than many African American men. . . . Women may be subject to the dual effects of racism and sexism and hence may be in double jeopardy" (Schiele, 1992, p. 52).

One might argue that both White women and minority women faculty are expected to perform similar activities in academia. Although it could be the case, White women faculty "can more easily say no" to demands such as performing service activities than minority women faculty

(Young, 1984, p. 136). As a result, minority women faculty experience the academic workplace differently from White women faculty. One could say that minority women faculty are more at risk because of the discriminating effects of gender than White women faculty. One could also say, as some researchers have noted, that the obstacles faced by minority women faculty in academia block their advancement in academia to a greater degree than similar obstacles block the advancement of White women faculty (Elmore and Blackburn, 1983; Carroll, 1973; Dejoie, 1977; Grillo, 1997; Menges and Exum, 1983; Young, 1996).

Issues in the Workplace for Minority Faculty

Similar to women faculty, minority faculty perceive little opportunity in the academic workplace to participate in institutional activities, especially activities that are crucial to establishing institutional presence (Aguirre, 1985; Jackson, 1991) such as serving on tenure and promotion committees or campus budget planning committees. Minority faculty also perceive themselves mainly as assigned to teach classes that serve a service component in their academic department (Aguirre, 1987; Haines, 1991; Tack and Patitu, 1992). In particular, minority faculty often find themselves assigned to teach classes that are general service classes but not required to satisfy the major in the department. The academic workplace "expects" minority faculty to assume responsibility for its service activities: "Minority faculty face significant role conflicts. . . . They must balance teaching, research, and service to the institution, knowing that there are pressures to perform in each area, though rewards are not equal. At the same time, they are also often given more chances to fill service responsibilities than their white peers—and they are expected to take them" (Exum, 1983, p. 395).

A study of Latino faculty members' attitudes about the workplace (Martinez, Hernandez, and Aguirre, 1993) found that Latino faculty perceive few opportunities in the academic workplace for assuming leadership roles or positions with the potential for leadership. In contrast, White faculty perceive the academic workplace as open to anyone interested in pursuing leadership roles or positions. "Latino faculty are more likely to perceive minority faculty as excluded from mainstream decision-making sectors on campus and channeled into buffer statuses where they are used to protect institutional interests" (p. 48). In this case, Latino faculty are likely to perceive themselves as part of the academic workplace if their presence serves and protects institutional interests. For example, the institution can "window dress" its minority faculty to respond to critics that accuse it of not having any minority faculty.

An examination of "quality of life" in the academic workplace for White and Black faculty in predominantly White schools of social work (Davis, 1985) found that Black faculty perceived barriers in the academic workplace that prevented them from receiving respect and attaining job satisfaction. In particular, Black faculty perceived themselves as less respected in the academic workplace, as less likely to receive satisfaction from their academic positions, and with less certain employment futures than White faculty. Davis suggests that the cumulative effect of these perceptions on minority faculty serves as a vehicle that motivates Black faculty to leave their academic positions. The cumulative effect of these perceptions also prevents minority faculty from attaining a quality of life similar to the one attained by White faculty.

Although this review of the research literature shows that minority faculty perceive barriers in the academic workplace, studies in the research literature also show that minority faculty perceive the workplace environment as supportive of their professional growth and socialization. A study of minority faculty and their perceptions of conditions in the workplace in U.S. schools of social work (Grandbois, Andrews, and Schadt, 1996) found that minority faculty perceived the academic workplace as supporting the hiring of minority faculty and their career objectives. Similarly, a study of minority faculty and perceptions of their quality of life in the academic workplace (Thomas and Asunka, 1995) found that minority faculty are generally satisfied with their quality of life in the academic workplace. Another study of quality of life for minority faculty (Tack and Patitu, 1992) observes that although minority faculty generally perceive the academic workplace as supportive of their career goals, they also believe that the academic workplace does not adequately use their skills and experiences. For example, minority faculty perceive the academic workplace as using them selectively, based on their minority status, to serve on service and affirmative action committees.

The Institutional Context

What are the institutional factors that shape women's and minority faculty members' perceptions of the workplace? If women and minority faculty perceive barriers in the academic workplace regarding their job satisfaction, career opportunities, and professional mobility, then how can the workplace alter their perceptions about barriers in the workplace? Perhaps by examining how the workplace organizes the perceptions of women and minority faculty, we can identify institutional factors that women and minority faculty perceive as barriers. Despite the paucity of studies that examine institutional factors as barriers for women and minority faculty, a few studies have attempted to describe the institutional context for women's and minority faculty members' participation in the academic workplace.

Grandbois and others (1996) conducted a survey of minority faculty perceptions regarding selected workplace conditions in U.S. schools of social work. The survey examined institutional efforts to hire minority faculty, minority faculty perceptions of institutional success in hiring minority faculty, conduciveness and supportiveness of the workplace for minority faculty career goals, institutional opportunity for minority faculty to influence decision making and assume leadership roles, and perceived racism and harassment by colleagues and students. In general, the survey results showed that minority faculty perceived the academic workplace as supportive regarding the hiring of minority faculty and their career objectives. "When asked whether their minority status was an endangerment, advantage, disadvantage or asset, 6% (13) reported an endangerment, 13% (28) an advantage, 45% (100) neither an advantage or disadvantage, and 18% (39) . . . an asset" (p. 650).

Table 11 shows the reconfigured results presented by Grandbois and others (1996). The table shows that minority faculty perceive the school's working environment, administrators, and faculty as supportive of their career objectives. What do these results suggest about the institutional context for minority faculty? On the one hand, the results identify a set of institutional factors—the school's working environment, administrative and faculty support—that minority faculty perceive as important to the attainment of their career objectives. On the other hand, the results identify a set of institutional factors

TABLE 11
Minority Faculty Responses to Select Institutional Factors*

Institutional Factor		Minority Faculty Response	
		Always/ Usually	Seldom/ Never
Conduciveness of over-all	%	76	24
working environment of	N	113	35
the school			
Supportiveness of dean in	%	84	16
helping achieve their	N	142	28
[minority faculty] objectives			
Supportiveness of faculty	%	54	46
(as a group) in helping	N	76	65
achieve their [minority			
faculty] objectives			

*Adapted from Table 1 in Grandbois and others (1996: 649).

that could be perceived by faculty as *barriers* to the attainment of their career objectives. Banks (1984), for example, notes that the entry of Black scholars into predominantly White American universities resulted in an institutional context that offered *service* as a vehicle for institutional participation but ended up as a barrier to their career advancement:

> *The administrators of universities expected black scholars to function quite differently from their white counterparts. . . . Rather than being allowed—and indeed encouraged—to concentrate on their academic work, many black professors were sucked into a plethora of activities often unrelated to their competence and interests. Institutions that had traditionally discouraged younger faculty members from participating on administrative committees and in community affairs drafted young black scholars for these activities. . . . Consequently, many individuals who had been trained for serious intellectual work and took jobs expecting to do such work found that their orientation was not compatible with what the institutions expected of them.* (pp. 326–327)

Similarly, an examination of Black faculty attitudes and perceptions of the academic workplace (Tack and Patitu, 1992) found that Black faculty generally perceive the academic work environment as supportive of their career goals. Although Black faculty perceive select institutional factors—department and campus working relationships, identification with department and institution—as supportive of their presence in the academic workplace, the majority of Black faculty believe that the institution could better use their skills and experiences. In particular, because Black faculty perceive little opportunity to serve on important committees, they may believe that the workplace uses their skills and experiences selectively. That is, Black faculty may perceive the workplace as using them selectively regarding their minority status in the academic workplace. According to Tack and Patitu, "Minorities perceive their chances as being better than those of whites for service on committees that make decisions about affirmative action and student affairs. Only one-fourth of the professionals, however, thought that service on affirmative action committees assisted them in achieving promotion and tenure" (p. 69). Thus, selective use of minority faculty based on their minority status in the academic workplace may serve as a barrier to the career objectives of minority faculty (Garza, 1988; Washington and Harvey, 1989). As such, minority faculty may be caught in an *ethnic mobility trap*—by responding to workplace opportunities that use their minority status, minority faculty are shielded from more rewarding opportunities in the academic workplace (for a discussion of the ethnic mobility trap, see Aguirre, 1987; Wiley, 1967).

Finally, Niemann and Dovidio (1998) examined the association between solo status of racial and ethnic minority faculty in psychology departments with their job satisfaction and subjective feelings of distinctiveness. In general, the solo status ("being the only one") experienced by racial and ethnic minority faculty was expected to be associated with level of job satisfaction and feelings of distinctiveness. The findings show that minority faculty generally report lower levels of job satisfaction than White faculty. For minority faculty, job satisfaction was affected or mediated by their feelings of distinctiveness. That is, solo minority faculty exhibited higher levels of distinctiveness that in turn resulted in lower levels of job satisfaction. In contrast, nonsolo minority faculty exhibited low levels of distinctiveness that in turn resulted in higher levels of job satisfaction. Interestingly, the level of distinction experienced by a minority faculty member may increase his or her perceived vulnerability to negative stereotypes in the academic workplace. According to Niemann and Dovidio:

Perceptions of minorities being treated inequitably may lead to feelings of distinctiveness as a function of one's race or ethnicity for minorities. In turn, feelings of distinctiveness may sensitize minorities to the potential for being singled out for unfair treatment. Thus, in complex, naturalistic settings involving interactions over time, feelings of distinctiveness and stigmatization may represent a reinforcing, circular phenomenon. (p. 67)

The solo status of minority faculty has built-in obstacles. For example, according to the fictional law professor Geneva Crenshaw:

When I arrived [the first black hired], the white faculty members were friendly and supportive. They smiled at me a lot and offered help and advice. When they saw how much time I spent helping minority students and how I struggled with my first writing, they seemed pleased. Then after I became acclimated to academic life, I began receiving invitations to publish in the top law reviews, to serve on important commissions, and to lecture at other schools. At this point, I noticed that some of my once-smiling colleagues now greeted me with frowns. . . . The more successful I appeared, the harsher became the collective [judgment] of my former friends. (Bell, 1987, p. 157).

The solo status of minority faculty may also threaten the expectations White faculty have for him or her:

At first, the white professor feels good about hiring the minority. It shows how liberal the white is, and the minority is assumed to want nothing more than to scrape by in the rarified world they both inhabit. But the minority does not just scrape by, is not eternally grateful, and indeed starts to surpass the white professor. This is disturbing; things weren't meant to go that way. (Richard Delgado, quoted in Bell, 1995, pp. 896–897)

Fitting In in the Academic Workplace

Women and minority faculty share similar perceptions of barriers in the academic workplace to their professional growth and socialization. Women and minority faculty generally regard the barriers as the product of an organizational culture that serves the interests of White male faculty (Bell, 1986; Hughes, 1998; Ware, 2000). An outcome of these barriers for women and minority faculty is that they acquire a "distinctiveness" in the academic workplace that has negative outcomes for them. In turn, the distinctiveness they acquire in the academic workplace puts women and minority faculty in a context of role entrapment: They belong in the academic workplace but only under certain conditions (Kanter, 1977; Milliken and Martins, 1996). As a result, women and minority faculty often perceive themselves as "tokens," "curiosities," or "anomalies" in the academic workplace (Delgado, 1991; Yoder, 1985).

According to Moore (1982), women are perceived as "curiosities" in the academic workplace because their entry into higher education was limited to subservient roles. The entry of women into higher education, for example, was often confined to the areas of homemaking and home economics. "[Accommodations] were made to meet the presumed needs and abilities of women in most colleges. For example, domestic work such as cooking, washing, and ironing [was] delegated to them at such colleges as Mount Holyoke and Oberlin" (p. 217). The context of "domesticity" created for women in higher education also served as a vehicle for recruiting women into academic teaching positions. As such, women were tracked into academic teaching positions that were subservient in academia and did not pose a threat to men faculty. It is not surprising to find that, as a result, men faculty regarded women faculty as curiosities and in some cases as irritants (Moran, 1986).

Minority faculty are "anomalies" in the academic workplace because they are expected to be model citizens (Delgado, 1991). Minority faculty are expected to be "super minorities"—to be different from other members of their

> *Women and minority faculty generally regard the barriers to their professional growth and socialization as the product of an organizational culture that serves the interests of White male faculty.*

minority group. For example, minority faculty are often told by White faculty: "You are so different from other members of your group." Consequently, the academic workplace expects minority faculty to be "shining examples" or role models of academic citizenship. Minority faculty can be part of the academic workplace only if they exhibit in their behavior the expectations set for them. In this sense, minority faculty can have a "minority" identity but not a "personal" one.

With regard to the institutional role of minority faculty in the academic workplace, minority faculty perceive White faculty as *gatekeepers* that constantly monitor their behavior:

> *Another factor that troubles many black faculty is the institutional environment in which they find themselves when they do get a position in a predominantly white institution. Blacks are well aware, as are most outsiders, that they exist in a fishbowl, having their competence and behavior routinely and unofficially evaluated by most of the persons with whom they come in contact. They feel that they are expected to be shining examples of civic virtue.* (Moore, 1987–88, p. 121)

Consequently, minority faculty may perceive themselves as occupying a contradictory role in the academic workplace— *outsiders* but expected to be *model citizens* in academe.

Similarly, Arce (1976, 1978) has argued that not only are minority faculty *outsiders* in the academic workplace but also are often ascribed institutional roles that protect the interests of White faculty. In particular, Chicano faculty (but also other minority faculty) are *colonized* by the academic workplace to subscribe to an ideology that does not promote their personal growth but instead forces them to accept institutional roles that protect White interests. One institutional role ascribed to Chicano faculty, for example, is rooted in an *affirmative action pattern:*

> *A number of Chicanos have been incorporated into specialized "Chicano roles" in many colleges and universities as part of the affirmative action response of the institutions. Though the principle of effective affirmative action that affects all levels and roles of an institution is very important and valuable, there has*

developed a mentality of being a professional, institutionalized Chicano. This mentality, whether formalized as a role filled by some Chicano staff or simply pursued as an advocatory approach, is here called the affirmative action pattern. . . . Chicanos that have these Chicano-role-specialties usually are located in the periphery of the decision-making and academic activities of colleges and universities. (Arce, 1978, p. 95)

By occupying the institutional roles ascribed to them in the academic workplace, minority faculty are thus meeting one institutional expectation, and their institutional role is not structurally integrated in the academic workplace (see also Hu-DeHart, 1983; Williams, 1978; and Brown, 1990, for a discussion of how the roles women and minority faculty occupy in the academic workplace victimize their gender or race and ethnicity).

Finally, Bronstein (1993) conducted a series of interviews with women and minority faculty to examine their general perceptions of their academic workplace and their roles in the academic workplace. Bronstein notes that the majority of persons she interviewed "reported that they had experienced racial and/or gender discrimination during their academic careers, often from both administration and department colleagues" (p. 67). Interestingly, the persons Bronstein interviewed remarked that their degree of *differentness* from White heterosexual males ("the mainstream model") affected the role they played and the treatment they received in the academic workplace. According to Bronstein, "the more 'different' people were, in comparison with that mainstream model, the more difficult a time they had in their institutions, particularly on a personal level" (p. 68).

In addition, the *differentness* of women and minority faculty can pose a threat to White male faculty. For example, students', especially graduate students', interest in feminist and multicultural issues can result in their demand for the teaching and mentoring services of women and minority faculty. White male faculty would, as a result, find less demand for their services in the academic workplace. The *differentness* of minority and women faculty can thus place them in institutional roles that have the potential of changing the academic workplace.

Feminist and ethnic minority scholars can present a threat to the status and privilege of white male faculty. What the respondents in this study universally reported was success with students: high demand and appreciation for the courses they taught, and for their services as advisers and mentors. Such responses from the "customers" in academic institutions have the eventual effect of shaping the curriculum, which means that those teaching the traditional offerings may find their services less valued and less in demand. . . . White male faculty may feel that their own evaluations will suffer, in comparison with popular feminist and ethnic minority teachers. (Bronstein, 1993, p. 68)

Organizational Fit

According to Olsen, Maple, and Stage (1995), the association between organizational values and personal values can be used to examine the organizational fit of women and minority faculty in the academic workplace: "The concept of 'fit' would appear to be usefully applied to groups such as women and minorities whose professional values (as expressed in their interests, satisfactions, and relative expenditure of time) are supposed to vary from the traditional white male model in consistent and predictable ways" (p. 271). Similarly, Chatman (1989) has suggested that organizational fit can be evaluated by examining the "congruence between norms and values of organization and the values of persons" (p. 339). Accordingly, Steers (1991) suggests that a person's perception of the place he or she occupies in the organization is a measure of organizational fit.

If women and minority faculty perceive barriers in the academic workplace that make them peripheral participants in institutional activities, then they have a weak fit in the academic workplace. The weak fit of women and minority faculty may facilitate their segmentation into workplace activities that are not expected of White male faculty (for a discussion of segmented labor markets in higher education, see Rosenblum and Rosenblum, 1990; and Smith and Hixson, 1987). As a result, women and minority faculty occupy a niche in the academic workplace that is typified by their gender and/or minority status and promotes their image as "tokens" or "anomalies" (Bellas and Toutkoushian, 1999; Merritt and Reskin, 1992, 1997). Russell (1995) offers a snapshot of the niche occupied by minority faculty in academia: "The presence of the black woman faculty member is a daily reminder that the law school as an institution has been adjudicated a practitioner of racial and gender discrimination, an immoral act of rank order. Her presence symbolizes the institution's contrition. . . . The tendency is to assume her inferiority, to believe that her appointment was unmerited, and was thus nothing more than a grant of their grace" (p. 499).

The weak organizational fit of women and minority faculty in the academic workplace, their *peripheralness* and *segmentation,* may also instruct us regarding their institutional representation. Nkomo (1992) has observed that minorities have not been studied within the organizational literature because "there was little awareness that racial minorities may have something to contribute to organization or that perhaps race can inform our understanding of organizations in other ways" (p. 500). One may suspect that women and minorities are relatively *invisible* within an organization, because they are not regarded as capable of making contributions to the organization, especially the academic workplace (see Moore, 1982; Exum, 1983). The invisibility of women and minorities in organizations is closely associated with their ability to network with other organizational members (Ibarra, 1993, 1995). Ironically, even in organizations where minorities represent the majority of members, such as Blacks in professional sports, minorities are absent from decision-making positions in the organizational structure, for example, executive positions in the front office of professional sports (Shropshire, 1996). Similarly, women and minorities find themselves invisible in the academic workplace because their research on feminist or minority topics is viewed as insignificant (Cox and Nkomo, 1990; Reyes and Halcon, 1988; Park, 1996). Thus, the *peripheralness* and *segmentation* of women and minority faculty in the academic workplace promotes their invisibility in academe.

Finally, other than the organizational dimensions of *peripheralness* and *segmentation,* what other organizational dimensions can one examine regarding the organizational fit of women and minority faculty in the academic workplace? Although the perceptions women and minority faculty have of their role in the academic workplace are important in determining organizational fit, Olsen and others (1995) propose two other organizational dimensions: (a) "self-efficacy or sense of personal control over one's career" (p. 272), and (b) "how much intrinsic reward faculty derive from their work" (p. 273). To examine the association of these two organizational dimensions with the organizational fit of women and minority faculty, Olsen and others conducted interviews with 146 tenure-track faculty at a Research I university: 70 (48%) male and 76 (52%) female, and 99 (68%) White and 47 (32%) minority faculty. In general, women and minority faculty tended to identify with university values emphasizing research and publication. The interviews with women faculty showed that women faculty "like their white male colleagues, tend to define themselves professionally in terms of their research, derive as much intrinsic reward from their academic work, and are satisfied with their research activities" (p. 283). The interviews with minority faculty showed that their pattern of role interests was different from other faculty because they "evidenced greater identification with, and satisfaction from, teaching than other groups of faculty" (p. 283). Thus:

> *In sum, the findings of the present study suggest that current assessments of women and minority faculty's role interests may be a less than accurate characterization, at least for faculty at a research-oriented institution. Further, of the different role measures used (identification with teaching/research roles, time allocation, and satisfaction), satisfaction with teaching and research proved most predictive of important aspects of institutional fit.* (p. 283)

One may thus approach an examination of how women and minority faculty fit in the academic workplace from several directions: by focusing on their participation in institutional activities, such as service in a university committee or occupying a leadership position; by focusing on how women and minority faculty perceive the alignment of their career goals with institutional expectations; and by examining how women and minority faculty perceive the allocation of rewards and opportunities in the academic workplace based on gender and/or minority status. The benefit of such a multidimensional approach to studying the organizational fit of women and minority faculty is that it facilitates the construction of a descriptive profile for women and minority faculty—a descriptive profile that portrays organizational dimensions as dynamic agents. By identifying organizational dimensions, one may in turn further the understanding of how the academic workplace can be structured to accommodate the organizational fit of women and minority faculty.

Summary

The discussion in this section has identified the precarious position of women and minority faculty in the academic workplace. Women and minority faculty share similar perceptions of barriers in the academic workplace to their professional growth and socialization. They perceive the academic workplace as chilly and alienating. Women and minority faculty share similar perceptions of themselves as tokens or curiosities in the academic workplace. These perceptions are reinforced by the observations made by women and minority faculty that the academic workplace segments their participation on the basis of gender and/or minority status.

The peripheralness and segmentation that characterize the participation of women and minority faculty in the academic workplace has identifiable outcomes. On the one hand, the institutional role of women and minority faculty is not structurally integrated in the academic workplace. That is, women and minority faculty are in an organizational niche that victimizes their gender and/or race and ethnicity. On the other hand, the institutional role of minority faculty places them in an ethnic mobility trap in the academic workplace. That is, the academic workplace uses the minority status of minority faculty to shield them from rewarding opportunities. Thus, both women and minority faculty have a weak organizational fit in the academic workplace.

ISSUES FACING WOMEN AND MINORITY FACULTY

Women and minorities find themselves in a workplace setting that favors the professional socialization of White male faculty. One outcome for women and minority faculty is that they encounter obstacles in the workplace to their professional socialization. In general, the obstacles target the gender and minority status of women and minority faculty. For example, women faculty are expected to be neutral, nonacting entities in the academic workplace. According to a White female faculty member describing her presence in a male-dominated workplace:

> *I smile, I am nice. I try to always feel like I am in a good humor and that I am not challenging anyone, but especially I smile, and it drives me nuts sometimes. If I did not smile or had the personality of some of my [male] colleagues I would be out on my ear. The men can get away with being nerds, but there is no way I could get away with that, even if I wasn't doing feminist things.* (quoted in Tierney and Bensimon, 1996, p. 82)

Similarly, Contreras (1995) describes the reception minority faculty receive in a workplace environment dominated by White faculty:

> *Just as cold, I discovered, was the social ambiance of the School of Education. After settling in I went to the campus and discovered that no one was expecting me. I had no office space nor any assignment for the semester. I quickly discovered that little was expected of me. I would be marginally involved in the core curriculum of my department. I was to be shared with various programs in addressing multicultural issues.* (p. 124)

Contreras's observation shows how integration into the academic workplace becomes problematic for minority faculty. Minority faculty are often expected to negotiate their way in the academic workplace without bothering anyone. It is not surprising then that minority faculty feel unwanted in the workplace.

This section examines institutional features of the academic workplace that women and minority faculty perceive to be barriers. Several questions serve as guides for the

Women and minorities find themselves in a workplace setting that favors the professional socialization of White male faculty.

discussion: What barriers do women and minority faculty encounter in the academic workplace? How do barriers in the academic workplace affect the professional socialization of women and minority faculty? How do women and minority faculty negotiate their identities in the academic workplace?

Barriers in the Academic Workplace

Workplace stressors create a context for academic work that requires faculty to juxtapose personal obligations and workplace tasks (McMillen, 1987; Gmelch and others, 1984, 1986). Faculty experience numerous stressors in the workplace:

> Job content *stressors . . . are centered on workload, decision making under ambiguity, and meeting self-imposed deadlines. The main* organizational *stressors are job complexity, role ambiguity, and role conflict.* Outside of work, *the major issue that puts pressure on faculty is the discrepancy between workplace tasks and family obligations; [they] can take many forms, especially among faculty who are married.* (Smith and others, 1995, p. 265)

The manner in which faculty respond to workplace stressors determines how they perceive their role in and identify with the workplace (Plater, 1995; Mooney, 1988). Workplace stressors are also an impediment to the professional socialization of faculty (Blackburn and Lawrence, 1995; Dey, 1994).

> *Stress appears to play an important role in the lives of university faculty. This fact has implications in the classroom and in research for the quality of faculty work. If faculty members are experiencing stress when attempting to accomplish tasks and likewise feel conflict over their roles within the university and at home, it is probable that their work will suffer.* (Smith and others, 1995, p. 279)

The extent to which workplace stressors affect faculty's performance of tasks in the workplace "can cause faculty members to become discouraged; in many cases, disgruntled faculty look elsewhere for a suitable working environment" (Tack and Patitu, 1992, p. 17). In particular, if workplace stressors prevent faculty members from performing workplace tasks satisfactorily, then professional socialization, such as promotion and tenure, is disrupted.

Table 12 shows how White and minority faculty respond to sources of stress in the academic workplace. In general, women faculty have higher responses to sources of stress in the workplace than men faculty. Interestingly, the one source of workplace stress for which men faculty have a higher response than women faculty has to do with research or publishing demands. It may be that women faculty have a lower response to research and publishing demands as a source of stress because they perceive the institutional rewards, such as tenure and promotion, associated with research and publishing are fewer for women than for men (Creamer, 1998; Gmelch and others, 1986; Witt and Lovrich, 1988). In contrast, women faculty have a higher response than men faculty to teaching load as a source of stress because they often find themselves burdened with classes with large enrollments and performing supplemental teaching activities, such as advising women students (Clark and Corcoran, 1986; Phillips, 1993; DiNitto and others, 1995). As such, teaching activities may carry greater weight for

If workplace stressors prevent faculty members from performing workplace tasks satisfactorily, then professional socialization, such as promotion and tenure, is disrupted.

TABLE 12

Sources of Stress for White and Minority Faculty, 1995–1996

Sources of Stress	White Faculty		Minority Faculty[1]	
	Men	Women	Men	Women
Time Pressures	83%	93%	76%	90%
Lack of Personal Time	77%	91%	74%	86%
Teaching Load	60%	71%	61%	66%
Review/Promotion Process	41%	49%	52%	55%
Research/Publ. Demands	50%	47%	50%	47%
Child Care	32%	33%	36%	31%
Subtle Discrimination	15%	32%	47%	51%

[1]minority faculty = Black, Latino, Asian, American Indian

Source: special tabulation, "Race and Ethnicity in the American Professoriate, 1995–96," UCLA Higher Education Research Institute.

women than for men in the peer-review process found in the workplace. Astin and Davis (1985) summarize the difference between men and women faculty to workplace stress: "Men identify as inhibitors those situations over which they have less personal control (i.e., availability of funds, student help, or institutional support), whereas women indicate as inhibitors those situations in which they could exercise greater control (i.e., involvement in teaching, committee work, or family tasks)" (p. 151).

According to Table 12, White and minority women faculty are more likely than men faculty to experience subtle discrimination as a source of stress in the academic workplace. The research literature suggests that women faculty are more likely than men faculty to be victims of subtle discrimination, such as men faculty members' negative views of women faculty as inept or incompetent (Gallant and Cross, 1993; Henry, 1990). In particular, qualities that are positively associated with men faculty are often negatively associated with women faculty: "What is forthright and bold in men is considered aggressive and bitchy—and noncollegial—in women" (Toth, 1995, p. 46).

Minority status compounds the subtle discrimination experienced by minority women faculty in the academic workplace. According to McCombs (1989), the minority status of Black women faculty results in social processes that alienate and isolate them in the academic workplace. Similarly, Nieves-Squires (1992) observes that the minority status of Hispanic women faculty is used in the academic workplace to segment them into service activities that target Hispanic students. Minority women faculty are also more likely than White women to find themselves the victims of negative stereotypes in the academic workplace (Menges and Exum, 1983; Young, 1984; Fontaine and Greenlee, 1993). For example, White faculty often regard the presence of minority women faculty in the workplace as the product of affirmative action. As such, White faculty regard their presence as the outcome of avoiding considerations of merit and focus instead on their minority status.

Workplace Issues
The research literature on women and minority faculty suggests that they are less satisfied with the workplace than White men faculty. Women's and minority faculty members'

satisfaction with the workplace is also affected by the barriers they encounter in the workplace. The barriers encountered by women and minority faculty are *workplace issues* for them because they affect their professional socialization and career opportunities in the academic workplace. These workplace issues are important to our understanding of why women and minority faculty perceive themselves in an anomalous position in the academic workplace (Aguirre and others, 1994). The distinction of often being the "only one" in the workplace results in minority faculty members' having lower levels of job satisfaction than white faculty (Niemann and Dovidio, 1998). In some cases, the organizational context of the academic workplace portrays minority women faculty as anomalies: "When Latinas gain entry or are hired in higher education, suspicion about the reasons for their being there are raised as a form of tokenism or as examples of reverse discrimination" (Montero-Sieburth, 1996, p. 70).

Gendered salary

One of the workplace issues women faculty cite most often has to do with the presence of differentials in faculty pay (Pounder, 1989; Kelly, 1989; Toutkoushian, 1998; Alpert, 1989; Barbezat, 1987; Luna, 1990). According to Hensel (1991), the American Association of University Professors has found that, since 1975, the salary gap between men and women faculty has not narrowed and that it, in fact, has expanded at the assistant professor level. Regarding entry-level salaries (e.g., assistant professor rank) for women faculty, Bellas (1997) has observed that the number of women in an academic discipline has a negative nonlinear effect on entry-level salaries: "The strongest effect . . . on average disciplinary salary appears to occur among disciplines that have less than 15–20% women; the negative effect weakens among disciplines with greater proportions of women, although a negative effect remains" (p. 315).

Ransom and Megdal (1993) examined the relative pay of men and women faculty between 1965 and 1985 to see whether affirmative action initiatives such as the Equal Pay Act of 1963 decreased salary differentials between men and women faculty. In general, they found that affirmative action initiatives had increased the representation of women on college and university faculties and their salaries relative to men's salaries between the late 1960s and early 1970s. Despite the relative increase in salary for women faculty, however:

> *Since 1977, the relative pay of women apparently has not improved. . . . Equal pay policies do not seem to have been too effective in higher education. By our estimates, women faculty members are, on average, paid significantly less than equally capable men. Nationally, relative pay of women probably did not improve in the late 1970s and early 1980s. (p. 34)*

Is *gender* the primary variable that creates a context of gendered income for women faculty? That is, can the salary differences between men and women faculty be explained by examining other factors such as career experience, education, publications, and research? Bognanno (1987) suggests that although factors such as the number of publications and time spent on research can explain some of the difference between men and women faculty salaries, the salary difference remains partially based on gender. Robin and Robin (1983) examined a series of comprehensive salary researches between 1977 and 1980 to identify variables that describe the context for differentials in women and men faculty salaries. They analyzed their data by means of a multiple classification scheme that focused on six independent variables: academic rank, college of employment (social sciences, natural sciences, etc.), sex, race, highest degree earned, and years in academic rank. In general, Robin and Robin found that even when they controlled for some of the independent variables, a salary differential existed between women and men faculty:

> *The data [indicate] that, during the first two years researched, women were found to receive lower salaries than the average at all ranks. The multiple classification analysis, controlling for the salient variables identified through the multiple stepwise regression analysis, indicated that the salary decrements for women faculty persisted even when the factors of rank, race, college, highest degree, and years in rank were adjusted for. (p. 54)*

Similarly, Ervin, Thomas, and Zey-Ferrell (1984) tested the thesis that inequities based on sex exist in the academic workplace. To test the thesis, they constructed a model consisting of 10 background variables (sex, age, race, marital status, highest degree earned, length of time with doctorate, years employed by the university, institutional category [Carnegie Type I, II, etc.], academic discipline, and ideal workstyle [teaching x research x service]), 6 work activity variables (actual workstyle [teaching x research x service], chair's perception of faculty workstyle, time spent in teaching, time spent in research, time spent in service, and total time spent working), and 7 productivity variables (obtaining external grants, obtaining internal grants, release time received, number of published monographs, number of published articles in distinguished-quality journals, number of published articles in intermediate-quality journals, and number of published articles in low-quality journals). Ervin and others used their model to examine the predictive effects of the background variables, work activity variables, and productivity variables on four types of reward in the academic workplace: tenure, rank, salary, and type of appointment (nontrack, part time, etc.).

In general, Ervin and others (1984) found that of the four types of rewards they examined, only salary differed by sex. Their results showed that men faculty earn significantly more than women faculty (about $130.37 per month more) and that men faculty are more likely to receive rewards for achieved characteristics than women faculty. "It can be seen readily that sex, in this case femaleness, is negatively related (−.10) to salary. Stated another way, after we . . . controlled for longevity, discipline, and other predictors of salary, women earn less than men" (p. 1019).

The research literature thus suggests that gender plays a role in salary differences between women and men faculty. Salary differences between men and women faculty are a workplace issue because they affect job performance and job satisfaction. According to Hagedorn (1995), gender-based wage differentials in academia tend to decrease job satisfaction, increase work-related stress, and increase negative perceptions of collegiality among women faculty. Similarly, Pfeffer and Langton (1993) note that in general salary differentials between faculty have negative effects on job satisfaction and research productivity. Salary differentials between men and women faculty also have more financial consequences for women than for men (Astin and Bayer, 1972; Moses, 1997). For example, lower salaries for women faculty mean that it takes them longer to amass human capital, such as a salary base for computing retirement salaries, comparable to a man's.

Minority faculty salaries

The research literature is relatively silent regarding salary differentials between minority and nonminority faculty. Given the discriminating effects of minority status in U.S. society on educational outcomes, income, and occupation, however, one would expect to find salary differences between minority and nonminority faculty (for examples of how minority status operates as a discriminating dimension, see Aguirre and Turner, 1998). Finkelstein (1982) and Brasskamp (1978), for example, offer descriptive accounts of how minority status results in salary inequity between minority and nonminority faculty. In general, they note that minority faculty salaries are lower than those for nonminority faculty.

In a closer look at how minority status affects faculty salaries, Ford (1984) examined faculty pay in the School of Management at a medium-sized university in the Southwest. The objective of the study was to determine, by controlling for university service and academic rank, whether minority status affects faculty salaries. Of the 22 subjects in the study, all were full-time faculty, male, and had Ph.D. degrees; all had been at the university three years or more and had received at least two pay raises; and all but three were associate professors or professors. Seven were non-White (1 Black, 3 East Indians, and 3 Chinese). By using multiple regression analysis, Ford found that White faculty received, on average, $462 more than non-White faculty in annual salary increases and that White faculty earned, on average, $4,200 more per year than non-White faculty.

Pavel, Skinner, Cahalan, Tippiconnic, and Stein (1998) analyzed data from the Integrated Postsecondary Education Data System (IPEDS) for fall 1993 to study salary differentials between American Indian faculty and other faculty. They found that the median salary of American Indian faculty was about 91% of the salary earned by all full-time faculty. An examination of salary differentials by racial and ethnic population showed that American Indian faculty earned median salaries comparable to 81% of Asian faculty median salaries, 100% of Black faculty median salaries, 93% of Hispanic faculty median salaries, and 90% of White faculty median salaries. The data Pavel and others examined also showed that, in general, minority faculty earned 97% of the median faculty earned by White faculty. When Asian faculty were excluded from the minority population, however, the salary differential between White faculty and minority faculty was 92%. Accordingly, minority faculty earn lower salaries than White faculty and have lower rates of earning tenure than White faculty (Nettles and Perna, 1995).

In contrast, Russell (1991) found no appreciable salary differentials between minority and nonminority faculty (Table 13 summarizes the data examined by Russell). Table 13 shows that very small differences occur between the mean salaries of minority and nonminority faculty. One explanation for the lack of appreciable differences is found in the econometric literature arguing that minorities will receive high returns (e.g., salary) for signals of high productivity (e.g., postgraduate degrees). For example, minority persons who earn Ph.D. degrees would be expected to receive greater returns than a minority person without a Ph.D. degree—and perhaps even greater than a nonminority (White) person with a Ph.D. degree (Golbe, 1985). Freeman (1977b) found that Black male academics with publications to their credit earn more than their White counterparts. Similarly, Belman and Heywood (1991)

TABLE 13

Mean Incomes of Non-Minority and Minority Faculty by Type of Institution

Type of Institution	Total Income		Basic Salary	
	Non-Minority	Minority	Non-Minority	Minority
All Institutions	$48,931	$46,743	$39,501	$38,912
Doctoral	$60,981	$55,316	$47,735	$46,186
Other Four-Year	$40,450	$40,184	$33,938	$33,948
Source: Table V, Russell (1991).				

note that signals of high productivity (college and graduate school) are associated with higher returns for minorities. But:

> *It might be that the pattern of sheepskin effects results from a general "obstacles" model in which minorities achieve high levels of education only when they are unusually productive. Such an explanation implies minority earnings gaps should diminish with education levels and, correspondingly, that the minority return to additional years of education should be higher than that of white males which it isn't. The empirical results indicate minorities receive greater value from diplomas not from years of education.* (pp. 723–724)

Thus, there may not be any appreciable differences between the mean salaries of minority and nonminority faculty, because the Ph.D. degree reduces any *status distinction* between minority and nonminority faculty that could be translated into differential salary outcomes. That is, the Ph.D. degree, as a signal of high productivity, is translated in the academic workplace as a reduced earnings gap between minority and nonminority faculty.

A biased reward system

Although women faculty perceive themselves to be the victims of salary inequities, minority faculty perceive themselves to be the victims of a biased reward system. The presence of a biased reward system in the academic workplace is an important workplace issue for minority faculty because it affects their presence and permanence in academe. Seidman (1983), for example, conducted a series of in-depth interviews with 76 faculty and staff at community colleges in New York, Massachusetts, and California. The results showed that minority faculty believe they worked harder and were more conscientious in their work performance than White faculty to receive comparable rewards. According to Moore (1987–1988), minority faculty regard White faculty as gatekeepers in academia who control access to faculty ranks and the reward system. Minority faculty thus perceive themselves to be the victims of a biased reward system, finding it an obstacle to their presence and permanence in the academic workplace (Carter and O'Brien, 1993; Johnsrud, 1993; Fields, 1996).

One reward all faculty seek is tenure. Tenure not only endows the recipient with institutional permanency in academia but also serves as a signal for other faculty that the recipient's academic work is meritorious. The research literature notes the presence of obstacles in the academic workplace for minority faculty working toward tenure. The tenure review process required of faculty is often pregnant with discriminatory mechanisms that victimize minority faculty (Menges and Exum, 1983). For example, "Getting Tenure at the U" (Mindiola, 1995) describes a Chicano professor's involvement in a tenure dispute. A Chicano professor with a joint appointment in Chicano studies and an academic department underwent a tenure review by both departments.

In the end, the department voted six to five not to grant tenure. The recommendation was based upon there being an insufficient number of published scholarly articles. Chicano Studies, in contrast, strongly recommended the granting of tenure on the basis of outstanding service to the program and a more than acceptable record of scholarly achievement and publications, especially in light of the professor's dual responsibilities. (p. 33)

Minority faculty thus perceive themselves to be the victims of a biased reward system, finding it an obstacle to their presence and permanence in the academic workplace.

Although Mindiola notes in the essay that political factors were involved in the decision—another candidate came up for tenure at the same time in the same academic department, for example—the case study is instructive with regard to the risk of holding a joint appointment when it concerns institutional rewards such as tenure. In a sense, joint appointments become an obstacle for minority faculty members being reviewed for tenure because they have to meet two different sets of expectations. In some cases, such as the one described by Mindiola, the expectations are in conflict with each other. In contrast, majority (White) faculty members rarely face the conflict involved in trying to satisfy two different sets of expectations (Banks, 1984; Exum, 1983). Not surprisingly, academia attempts to sort minority faculty into joint appointments (Aguirre and Martinez, 1993; Garcia, 1978) and by doing so increases minority faculty members' chances of being turned down for tenure. As such, minority faculty are victims of a biased reward system that favors majority (White) faculty.

Women faculty

Women faculty are also victimized by a biased reward system in the academic workplace. According to Phillips (1993), women face a tenure trap in the academic workplace. In particular, the lack of personnel policies in the academic workplace that facilitate a women faculty member's having a family is an obstacle in women's pursuit of tenure. "There is an old joke that women should have their kids in the summer. . . . Men have children too, but they don't have the same problems as women" (p. 44). Ezrati (1983) notes that personnel policies in higher education adversely affect married women. In particular, single women faculty face fewer obstacles in the academic workplace than married faculty women with children. Similarly, Freeman (1977a) notes that married faculty women receive fewer institutional rewards than single faculty women or men faculty. According to Witt and Lovrich (1988), married women faculty often find themselves in a role conflict—dividing time between the academic workplace, and home and children. Time spent away from the academic workplace is perceived as an indication that a married woman faculty member is not serious about her career. This perception often appears during a married woman faculty member's tenure review (Hensel, 1991).

A study of women tenure-track assistant professors in a public Carnegie I research university (Finkel and Olswang, 1996) focused on women faculty members' perceptions of impediments and barriers in their careers. In general, the study's results showed that close to half the women faculty postponed having a child because they perceived it as an impediment to their professional interests and careers. "A large number of women assistant professors who choose to remain childless do so because of the perceived impact of children [on] their success in achieving tenure" (p. 131). If women faculty perceive childbearing as an impediment to their professional careers, then academia can lessen the perception of childbearing as an impediment by developing personnel policies—stopping the tenure clock, for example—that reduce conflict between personal and professional goals.

> *One primary policy solution is to grant tenure deferrals to all faculty members who become parents. . . . In this way, tenure pressure will be reduced. This policy recognizes that family obligations may affect productivity rates even for those individuals who continue to work immediately after a birth or otherwise limit their leaves. It is not unequal treatment to give faculty members who had a child the benefit of additional time to achieve tenure if they give birth during their probationary years; it is fair treatment.* (Finkel, Olswang, and She, 1994, p. 268)

Professional Socialization
The experiences of women and minority faculty in the academic workplace are different from those of White male faculty. Women and minority faculty are more likely than White men faculty to experience multiple sources of stress in the academic workplace that affect their professional socialization. For example, women and minority faculty might encounter social isolation (Yoder, 1985; Bell, 1986), a requirement to spend more time in service and teaching than White male faculty (Russell, 1991; Aguirre, 1987), discredited research (Reyes and Halcon, 1988; Parson and others, 1991), and fewer institutional rewards than White men faculty (Ervin and others, 1984; Exum, Menges, Watkins, and Berglund, 1984). The experience of women and minority faculty with these factors often results in their leaving the academic workplace (Rausch and others, 1989; Aguirre and Martinez, 1993). How do these factors affect the professional socialization of women and minority faculty?

Social isolation
Women and minority faculty are usually found in a peripheral position in the academic workplace. Sometimes being the only one in an academic department or college enhances the social isolation felt by women and minority faculty (Moran, 1986; Phelps, 1995). The social isolation experienced by women and minority faculty in the academic workplace affects their professional socialization; it excludes them from interacting with

information and support networks in the academic workplace that are important to obtaining resources and rewards (Clark and Corcoran, 1986; Banks, 1984). In particular, the social isolation experienced by women and minority faculty is an obstacle to their development of mentoring relationships and activities that could promote their success in the academic workplace (Parson and others, 1991; Carter, 1982). Thus, the social isolation experienced by women and minority faculty in the academic workplace prevents them from participating in and developing roles in the workplace similar to those of White men faculty.

Service and teaching

Because they are often the only one in their academic department or college, women and minority faculty find themselves performing more service activities than White men faculty, such as advising or serving on committees that focus on women and/or minority students (Rausch and others, 1989; Aguirre and Martinez, 1993). One result is that women and minority faculty find themselves overburdened with the demands of such service activities (Wyche and Graves, 1992). Women and minority faculty are also assigned more often to teach undergraduate classes than White men faculty (Menges and Exum, 1983; Johnsrud and Des Jarlais, 1994). And because women and minority faculty often have joint academic appointments, they are expected to assume responsibility for developing the curriculum and teaching the classes on women and minorities (Toth, 1995; McKay, 1995). Thus, compared with White men faculty, women and minority faculty spend more time in workplace activities such as teaching and service that do not necessarily promote their professional socialization in the academic workplace, especially the professional socialization that increases their chances of attaining tenure and promotions.

Discredited research

Regarding the acceptance of minority research, especially by White academics, Reyes and Halcon (1991) note:

> *The delegitimization of minority research by majority faculty is rooted in the values that [undergird] academe*

*and that are characteristic of culturally monolithic
systems. Those systems judge the quality of scholarship
from the normative perspective of their own cultural
group and thus deem deviations from the norm as
inferior.* (p. 176)

Similarly, Toth (1995) observes that women faculty are
advised, especially by men faculty, to limit their involvement
in feminist research until they have received tenure:

*Some young women are advised to postpone childbear-
ing and feminist research until after they have tenure.
They're told to write on subjects to which they're not
committed, to wait in silence and cunning until the
tenure decision is made.* (p. 45)

By discrediting feminist and minority research, the academic workplace reinforces the peripheral position of
women and minority faculty and questions the legitimacy of
their presence in academe (Chepyator-Thomson and King,
1996; Astin and Davis, 1985). In discrediting their research,
academia also negates the professional socialization of
women and minority faculty, especially their membership
in a community of scholars (Ayer, 1984; Haney-Lopez, 1991).
That is, women and minority faculty receive the
message that their research is not worthy of merit and, as a
result, does not legitimate their inclusion in the academic
community.

For example, Linda Mabry, an African-American female
law professor, quit the faculty of the Stanford Law School
because she was excluded by her colleagues from discussions concerning the creation of an international business
law program. Mabry saw the exclusion as a professional
insult because her area of expertise is international business
law. According to Mabry, the exclusion "was demoralizing
and embarrassing. . . . It was as if I were invisible" (quoted
in Mangan, 1999, p. A12). Her exclusion can be viewed as a
reflection of the institutional view.

Smaller institutional rewards
Based on our review of the research literature, we have
observed that women and minority faculty receive smaller
and fewer institutional rewards than White men faculty. In a

sense, this finding is not surprising. If women and minority faculty are spending more time than White men faculty in teaching and service and their research is discredited in the academic workplace, then women and minority faculty are destined to receive smaller and fewer institutional rewards, especially if one considers that they are excluded from pathways enjoyed by White men faculty that result in institutional rewards (Steward and others, 1995; Menges and Exum, 1983). In particular, by spending more time on service and teaching than White men faculty, women and minority faculty are limited in the amount of time they can spend in research. That is, their participation in research that could result in published articles is limited (Johnsrud and Des Jarlais, 1994; Olsen and others, 1995). In short, limits on the time they can devote to publishing and research decreases the access of women and minority faculty to institutional rewards, especially tenure.

Negotiated Identities

Given the barriers women and minority faculty encounter in the academic workplace, how do they negotiate their identities in academe? One response from women and minority faculty is to show that they are equal to White men faculty. Minority faculty, for example, place pressure on themselves "to prove that they are as good as white academics" (Reyes and Halcon, 1991, p. 174). This observation suggests that minority faculty attempt to negotiate their identity in the academic workplace by proving that they are equal to White faculty. The dilemma for minority faculty in accepting this practice is that they must be overachievers in a context where White faculty are not themselves overachievers. The dilemma is compounded if one considers that minority faculty must undergo an "acculturative" rather than a "socialization" process to mirror the behavior of White faculty (Contreras, 1998). That is, minority faculty must change their identities as well as their professional goals to match those of White faculty. In the end, minority faculty may displace themselves farther from the academic workplace.

Perhaps the most serious dilemma that women and minority faculty face in the academic workplace is the notion of *tokenism*. Montero-Sieburth (1996) suggests that the use of affirmative action policies in academia to increase the representation of women and minority faculty has often resulted in their portrayal as tokens or examples of reverse discrimination. It is possible that the academic workplace enhances the tokenism of minority faculty, for example, by segmenting them into service activities that White faculty often do not perform.

> *I assert that in the current regime of tokenism [that] is characterized by an occasional professor of color in otherwise all white institutions, the university and the community subject a professor of color to conflicting demands and disproportionately high service obligations. . . . Professors of color . . . are also expected to perform in symbolic roles and serve symbolic signifying functions. These disproportionate service obligations make it difficult for the professor of color to choose his own role and may hamper his effective performance of other important professorial responsibilities.* (Greene, 1991, pp. 297–298)

Similarly, the tokenism of women faculty is enhanced in the academic workplace when they are asked to use their intuitive sense of compassion to deal with students, especially women students. "An academic woman must also resist the compassion trap: being always available to everyone. Universities are full of needy students, and we do what we can for them, but no one person can be the adviser for all the women students" (Toth, 1995, pp. 42–43).

Perhaps one strategy that women and minority faculty can use to negotiate their identity regarding the concept of tokenism is to avoid participating in institutional activities that victimize their gender and/or minority status. Minority faculty can avoid service on university committees (such as affirmative action committees) that reinforce their identity as *minority* faculty and structure opportunity for them only in minority-oriented activities. Women faculty can avoid serving as academic advisers for all the women students in their department. Such segmentation by gender easily leads to the perception that academic advising is women's work. As such, both women and minority faculty can challenge the perception that they are tokens in the academic workplace.

Summary

Women and minority faculty experience the academic work-place differently from White men faculty. Because the academic workplace is organized to meet the professional needs of White men faculty, women and minority faculty encounter barriers to their professional socialization in the academic workplace—barriers such as how rewards like salary and tenure are allocated and social isolation, which constrains their ability to identify with and fit in the academic workplace.

The manner in which the academic workplace structures the participation of women and minority faculty can result in a dilemma for their identity in academia. By discrediting their research, academia questions the role of women and minority faculty. By segmenting their participation in the academic workplace into activities that victimize their gender and/or minority status, academia reinforces the tenuous relationship of women and minority faculty to the academic enterprise. In the end, women and minority faculty become victims when they are portrayed as tokens in the academic workplace.

SUMMARY OBSERVATIONS AND SUGGESTIONS

The workplace in U.S. society is predicted to become increasingly diverse in the 21st century (Johnston, 1987). Some believe that dramatic changes in the racial and ethnic composition of U.S. society will require comparable changes in the ethnic and racial composition of workers (Jordan, 1998). Others, however, believe that dramatic changes in the racial and ethnic composition of U.S. society will not improve diversity in the workplace but will instead foster exaggerated beliefs about workplace diversity (Gummer, 1998). What about workplace diversity for women and minority faculty in academia? The picture of women and minorities is not clear.

Diversifying the Faculty

There is no doubt that the representation of women and minorities in the faculty population increased between 1980 and 1993. While men increased their number in the faculty population by 5.1% between 1980 and 1993, women increased their number by 53.5%. In contrast, minorities increased by 56.1%, with minority women increasing by 84.6% and minority men by 42.9%. It appears then that women and minorities have made appreciable gains in their representation in the faculty population. Do these facts mean that academia has diversified its character? Does it mean that organizational change has taken place in academia?

Women faculty

Some researchers have suggested that the numerical gains made by women faculty are simply an outcome of their numerical increase in the student population and in the population of college degree recipients (Higgerson and Higgerson, 1991; Conway, 1989; Hensel, 1991). For example, between 1980 and 1990 the number of women students in higher education increased by 26%, while the number of men students increased by 7% (Aguirre, 1995a). In addition, between 1980 and 1990, the number of women awarded bachelor's degrees increased by 20%, the number of women awarded master's degrees increased by 9%, and the number of women awarded doctor's degrees increased by 42%. In contrast, figures for men were 1%, –3%, and –4%, respectively. As a result of increasing their number in the student population and in the number of degree recipients, especially doctor's degrees, women increased their numerical representation relative to men in the pool of available faculty.

Is the increased representation of women doctoral degree recipients in the pool of available faculty reflected in their numerical increase in the faculty population? According to the data we have examined, the number of doctoral degrees awarded to women between 1980 and 1993 increased 45.2%, while their number in the faculty population increased 53.5%. The data suggest that the numerical increase of women in the faculty population has kept pace with the number of women earning doctor's degrees. If women continue to increase the number earning doctor's degrees, then the faculty ranks will become increasingly diversified by women in the 21st century.

Minority faculty

Within the minority faculty population, Asians made the largest gain in number between 1980 and 1993. According to Sands and others (1992), the increase in the number of Asian faculty simply reflects a larger pool of available faculty than for Latinos or Blacks. Between 1980 and 1990, for example, the number of Asian students in higher education increased 94% (Aguirre, 1995a). In comparison, the number of Black students increased 10%, the number of Latino students 61%. With regard to the increase in degrees awarded between 1980 and 1990, the breakdown by racial and ethnic groups is as follows: bachelor's degrees—Asians (148%), Blacks (−4%), Latinos (48%); master's degrees—Asians (95%), Blacks (−16%), Latinos (42%); doctor's degrees—Asians (65%), Blacks (−16%), Latinos (42%). As a result, the gains made by Asians in the student population and in the awarding of degrees have expanded the pool of Asians available for faculty positions more than for Blacks or Latinos.

Special note must be made of the decreasing number of Blacks earning undergraduate and graduate degrees. On the one hand, the decreasing numbers of Blacks earning undergraduate and graduate degrees reflect the contextual relationship of Black persons to higher education (Washington and Newman, 1991), and the contextual relationship of Blacks to higher education reflects a shrinking pool of Black students progressing from high school to college

(Patton, 1988). On the other hand, the decreasing numbers of Blacks earning undergraduate and graduate degrees may explain why both Black men and Black women showed the smallest increase in the minority faculty population between 1980 and 1993. As a result, Black faculty may be overshadowed in the faculty population by Asians and Latinos. Comparatively speaking, however, Asians will become more noticeable in the faculty population in the 21st century than either Blacks or Latinos.

Institutional Initiatives

Another context may instruct us regarding the representation of women and minority faculty in academia—the outcome of *institutional initiatives* in academia that target diversity in the faculty ranks. As we have already noted, women and minorities made appreciable increases in the U.S. professoriat between 1980 and 1993. Moreover, the numerical increase of women and minorities in the faculty ranks between 1980 and 1993 was associated with the number of women and minorities earning doctoral degrees. What does this fact say about institutional initiatives in academe focused on faculty diversity?

Perhaps the single most controversial institutional initiative in academe designed to increase faculty diversity is *affirmative action.* If the purpose of affirmative action is to increase faculty diversity by drawing from a pool of available candidates, then affirmative action has satisfied its purpose. The data we have examined suggest that increases in the number of women and minority faculty have corresponded with their increase in the pool of available faculty. As such, it appears that affirmative action may have linked supply and demand. That is, the demand for women and minority faculty has kept up with the production of women and minorities earning doctoral degrees.

One must assume, however, that academia has been successful in promoting affirmative action initiatives that promote the graduate and professional education of women and minority faculty. The enrollment of women and minorities, for example, in graduate and professional education has been steadily increasing (Gose, 1996; Magner, 1997). Similarly, the proportion of women and minority faculty has been slowly increasing (Schneider, 1997). As a result, the number of women and minorities earning graduate degrees may serve as a vehicle in academia for the recruitment of faculty. If this is the case, then affirmative action is a signal that efforts to diversify the faculty have had results.

This is not to suggest that affirmative action has resolved the problems faced by women and minority faculty in academia. The reluctance of White faculty to discuss the discrimination faced by women and minority faculty limits the potential benefits of affirmative action in diversifying academia (Irvine and Walker, 1998; Smith, 1996; Stassen, 1995). In addition, the passage of anti–affirmative action legislation, such as Proposition 209 in California, and legal court cases that question the need for affirmative action programs in academia, such as *Hopwood v. Texas,* create a negative climate for affirmative action initiatives in academia (Rodriguez and Takaki, 1998; Gose, 1998; Malveaux, 1996). As a result, affirmative action is pregnant with social conflict in the academic workplace. According to Olivas (1988) with regard to Latino faculty, "unless higher education takes more seriously its responsibilities to seek out others like us, and to behave differently toward Latinos, the extraordinary cycle of exclusion from faculty ranks will continue. Higher education is poorer for its loss" (p. 9).

Suggestions

How can we enhance our understanding of faculty diversity in academia? The following questions can be used as guides for discussion.

1. What is the association between the number of women and minorities earning graduate degrees and their numerical representation in the faculty ranks? Does the numerical representation of women and minorities in the faculty population reflect their number earning graduate degrees?

2. Doc minority group representation in academia differ by racial and ethnic background? Are differences in minority groups in the faculty population associated with the groups' representation in the undergraduate and graduate student populations? Why are some minority groups not increasing their numbers as recipients of graduate degrees?

The reluctance of White faculty to discuss the discrimination faced by women and minority faculty limits the potential benefits of affirmative action in diversifying academia.

3. Is affirmative action an effective and adequate vehicle for recruiting women and minority faculty to academia? What institutional context has affirmative action created for women and minority faculty in academia?

Academic Culture and Diversity

Academic culture is, for the most part, hidden from the world outside the walls of academia. It is hidden not so much to hide its secrets as to promote the myth that knowledge is sacred. This explanation may help us understand why in popular thinking the academic culture is depicted as idyllic, a paradise free of conflict. We have noted, however, that the academic culture is characterized by conflict over resources and rewards. Struggles over power are fairly common in the academic culture. Such struggles, unfortunately, produce victims, persons who do not get tenure or whose research is not funded.

The academic culture shapes the perceptions of its subscribers—that is, the faculty. By examining faculty perceptions, one can construct a portrait of academic culture. Faculty perceptions are by no means homogeneous, however; they conflict with each other just as they are likely to complement each other. This outcome is not surprising if one considers that the academic culture is itself characterized by conflict. Faculty perceptions can thus instruct us regarding *what* brings academic culture together on a certain issue. For example, we noted earlier that "being a good teacher" and "being a good colleague" are important features of academic culture that a majority of the faculty share.

Diversity

Of particular interest is to observe how academic culture responds to institutional diversity. We examined faculty perceptions of academia's commitment to diversity; the examination showed that faculty generally perceive academia as committed to creating a diverse multicultural environment. In particular, faculty perceive this commitment as having increased between 1989–90 and 1995–96. Faculty perceive academia as increasing its support for the recruitment of women between 1989–90 and 1995–96 but decreasing its support for the recruitment of minorities. What do these findings have to say about the academic culture's response to diversity? Could it be that faculty perceive the academic culture is more responsive to women than to minorities?

Cortese (1992) has suggested that women, especially White women, have made greater gains than minorities because they have been more successful in lobbying for greater access. In particular, some researchers have noted that women have been successful at using affirmative action initiatives to gain access into academia (McMillen, 1986; Milem and Astin, 1993; Matthews, 1990; Schiele, 1992). If this is the case, then the academic culture may be more responsive to women than minorities. It must be noted that the academic culture may be responding to women because they have used networks as a vehicle for drawing the academic culture's attention. As such, women's efforts at networking may have resulted in an academic culture more responsive to their presence (McNeer, 1983; Carter, 1982; Wunsch, 1993).

What then must minorities do to alter the academic culture's perception of their presence? If networking is effective for women, then perhaps minorities would benefit from developing a network. For example, the University of Maryland–Baltimore County's Meyerhoff Program addresses the disparities in educational outcomes for Black males. The program's goal is to increase the number of Black faculty members, especially in engineering, medicine, and science. The program focuses on mentoring Black male students by Black male professionals, who serve as role models (Morgan, 1996).

Some researchers have suggested that minorities would benefit from mentoring activities that assist with the recruitment and retention of minorities into the faculty population (Mazingo, 1987; Nichols and Golden, 1982; Justus, 1987). Mentoring activities focused on minorities could also prompt the academic culture to recognize their growing presence in U.S. society (see, for examples, de los Santos, 1994; Luna and Cullen, 1995; Norman and Norman, 1995; Dickey, 1996; Jackson, 1996; McCormick, 1991). Minority mentoring activities could also play a role in shaping White faculty perceptions that support the inclusion of minorities in the faculty population (Stassen, 1995; Plata, 1996; Brinson and Kottler, 1993). Thus, mentoring activities can alter the academic culture's response to the inclusion of minorities in academe.

Although mentoring activities in academia can result in positive outcomes for minority faculty, they can have hidden pitfalls. For example, higher education institutions may be unwilling to provide the resources necessary for an effective mentoring program, or they may be unwilling to promote a mentoring program for minorities as a feature of the academic culture (Myers and Wilkins, 1995; Dickey, 1996). Minority women in faculty positions who could serve as mentors for minority women are in short supply (McCormick, 1991; Young, 1984; Ortiz, 1998). Moreover, mentoring activities may penalize minority faculty because White faculty do not regard them as vital to professional socialization, especially tenure and promotion (Blackwell, 1989; Brinson and Kottler, 1993).

Suggestions

The academic culture is a complex entity that shapes as well as alters the perceptions of its subscribers. The following questions are focused on enhancing our understanding of how the academic culture identifies diversity.

1. Do women and minority faculty occupy nested contexts in academia that segment them from White male faculty? Have mentoring activities initiated by women and minority faculty affected the perceptions held by White male faculty regarding their inclusion in academia?
2. How has the academic culture responded to mentoring activities for women and minority faculty? Have mentoring activities initiated by women and minority faculty affected the perceptions held by White male faculty regarding their inclusion in academia?
3. Will an increased presence of women and minority faculty affect faculty values regarding opportunity and rewards? That is, will an increased presence of women and minorities in the faculty population promote a multicultural system of opportunity and reward?

The Academic Workplace and Diversity

Despite an appreciable increase of women and minority faculty in the academic workplace, the academic workplace remains a *chilly* and *alienating* environment for women and minority faculty. One of the obstacles that women and minority faculty face is rooted in the ideological roots of the academic culture. That is, the academic culture of the academic workplace is designed to serve the interests of White men faculty. As a result, women and minority faculty are segmented into peripheral roles in the academic workplace, and they are excluded from participating in institutional activities that result in expanded opportunities and rewards.

Though we did not examine how the academic workplace affects women's and minority faculty members' perception of students' responses to their institutional presence, it deserves a brief note. We have examined how women and minority faculty identify barriers to their participation in the academic workplace. But how might these barriers affect students', especially white students', perception of women and minority faculty? One must keep in mind that just as the academic workplace is designed to meet the interests of White men faculty, academia is designed to meet the interests of White students (Feagin, Vera, and Imani, 1996; Allen, Epps, and Haniff, 1991; La Belle and Ward, 1996).

The research literature suggests that White students have biased perceptions of minority faculty (Aguirre, 1994). In general, White students perceive minority faculty as the products of affirmative action, and, as a result, they are marginalized in the eyes and thinking of White students. Patricia Williams (1991), a Black female law professor at Stanford, describes how she believes White students perceive her in class:

> *When some first-year law students walk in and see that I am their contracts teacher, I have been told, their whole perception of law school changes. . . . In the margins of their notebooks, or unconsciously perhaps, they deface me; to them, I "look like a stereotype of a black person" . . . not an academic. They see my brown face and they draw lines enlarging the lips and coloring in "black frizzy hair." They add "red eyes, to give . . . a demonic look." In the margins of their notebooks, I am obliterated.* (p. 115)

Williams's observation suggests that an academic culture designed by White students results in biased perceptions of minority faculty. Could it be that minority faculty receive a *chilly* reception from White students? Minority faculty may find themselves in a difficult position in the academic workplace, with White faculty and White students questioning their legitimate claim for presence in academia. One thus needs to examine how White faculty and White students perceive minority faculty in academia and how their perceptions are rooted in the academic culture.

Institutional presence

We have observed in our review of the research literature that the academic workplace uses women and minority faculty in selective activities. In particular, women and minority faculty are channeled into performing service activities in academia, such as advising women and/or minority students. The dilemma for women and minority faculty is that participation in service activities is often ignored in tenure and promotion decisions. Another dilemma for women and minority faculty is that their participation in service activities weakens their fit in the academic workplace. That is, women and minority faculty fit in the academic workplace when they perform service functions, but they do not fit into mainstream activities in academia controlled by White men faculty. As a result, the selective use of minority faculty in the academic workplace fosters "academic apartheid" by segmenting their participation in the academic culture (Contreras, 1998).

It is suggested that the weak organizational fit of women and minority faculty in the academic workplace reinforces their *peripheralness* and *segmentation* in the academic culture. The weak organizational fit of women faculty may partly explain why they become the targets of sex discrimination (Gray, 1985; Grunig, 1989) and why they become the targets of discrimination and racism (Brodie and Wiley, 1990; Elmore and Blackburn, 1983). The weak organizational fit for both women and minority faculty increases their chances of being victimized in the academic workplace. That is, women and minority faculty are victimized in the academic workplace because White men faculty perceive them as peripheral participants. In this sense, the academic workplace enhances the weak organizational fit of women and minority faculty.

Suggestions

Women and minority faculty may find themselves performing conflicting roles in the academic workplace. The academic workplace creates barriers for women and minority faculty that prevent them from receiving the same rewards and benefits as White men faculty. The following questions are designed to enhance our understanding of how women and minority faculty fit in the academic workplace.

1. What role do gender and minority status play in sorting women and minority faculty in the academic workplace? What is the purpose of the sorting process? Is it to protect the institutional interests of White men faculty?

2. How do women and minority faculty perceive White male faculty in the academic workplace? Does the academic culture support the perceptions White faculty and White students have for women and minority faculty?

3. Does the weak organizational fit of women and minority faculty increase their chances of being victimized in the academic workplace? What institutional initiatives can one introduce into the academic workplace that would strengthen the organizational fit of women and minority faculty as a means of reducing their level of victimization in the academic workplace?

Professional Socialization of Women and Minority Faculty

Women and minority faculty face barriers in their professional socialization in the academic workplace, including dimensions of stress that impede their role performance. Much of the workplace stress experienced by women and minority faculty results in role conflict for them. In particular, the social isolation experienced by women and minority faculty creates a context in the academic workplace that exposes them to discriminating treatment.

Two types of discrimination experienced by women and minority faculty are *unequal pay* and a *biased system of rewards.* Compared with White men faculty, women and minority faculty are underpaid and underrewarded. In a sense, the forms of discrimination experienced by women and minority faculty in the academic workplace reinforce the perceptions of White men faculty that women and

The social isolation experienced by women and minority faculty creates a context in the academic workplace that exposes them to discriminating treatment.

minorities are illegitimate participants in academia. The perceptions of women and minority faculty held by White men faculty also enhance their at-risk status in the academic workplace. Thus, women and minority faculty are at risk in the academic workplace because of the barriers they face regarding their professional socialization.

Competing perceptions

The barriers experienced by women and minority faculty regarding their professional socialization in the academic workplace have an observable outcome—competing perceptions of the academic workplace. Women and minority faculty perceive the academic workplace as biased against their research and publications and as unlikely to reward them, when compared with White men faculty, for their work. Unsurprisingly, the perception of a biased academic workplace often results in women's and minority faculty members' leaving the academic life. The unwillingness of the academic workplace to reward and recognize the work of women and minority faculty ends up forcing them out of the academic workplace.

If women and minority faculty decide to remain in the academic workplace, despite its barriers, then they must negotiate their identity in the workplace. In some cases, women and minority faculty negotiate their identity in the workplace by trying to be as good as White men faculty; in others, women faculty try to incorporate male behavioral orientations into their behaviors. The dilemma in trying to negotiate one's identity in this manner is that it ignores the underlying ideology of the academic workplace, and it is designed to meet the interests of White men faculty. Because they are perceived by White men faculty as tokens in the academic workplace, women and minority faculty work harder than White men faculty. Ironically, despite their efforts, White men faculty perceive them as meeting minimal expectations for faculty work. To compound the irony, White men faculty often treat their own minimal efforts as meeting maximum expectations for faculty work.

Suggestions

The data we have examined suggest that women and minority faculty are increasing their numerical representation in academia but that the barriers to professional socialization they experience impede their social presence in academia. The following questions are designed to guide an understanding of how women and minority faculty structure their participation in the academic workplace.

1. What types of barriers do women and minority faculty experience regarding their professional socialization in the academic workplace? How are these barriers legitimated by the academic culture? How does the academic culture facilitate the institutional continuity of these barriers?

2. What types of institutional initiatives need to be adopted to free women and minority faculty from unequal pay and a biased reward system? How do women and minority faculty use their faculty work—research and publications—to overcome unequal pay and a biased reward system? How do White men faculty use their work to legitimate unequal pay and a biased reward system?

3. How do women and minority faculty negotiate their social identities in the academic workplace? How are these negotiated social identities a response to the barriers experienced by women and minority faculty? How do White men faculty perceive the negotiated social identities of women and minority faculty?

A Final Note

This monograph uses the term *minority faculty* as a descriptive category for examining the academic workplace experiences of *non-White* faculty. By no means does the term indicate a perspective that non-White faculty are a homogeneous population, especially one with no internal variation. Instead, the term indicates two things in the research literature on minority faculty. First, the research literature focuses primarily on the experiences of Black and Latino faculty. As such, an implicit assumption in the research literature is that the experiences of all non-White faculty are similar to those of Black and Latino faculty. In a sense, the study of Black and Latino faculty has been by default considered the study of *minority* faculty. Thus, the term *minority faculty* in this monograph is a descriptor, much like a fisherman's net, for capturing *how* the minority faculty experience is described in the research literature.

Second, the term *minority faculty* incorporates non-White faculty into one descriptive category because the research literature on minority faculty is uneven in its examination of groups in the minority faculty population. Although a sizeable amount of research literature is available on Black and Latino faculty, there is very little regarding Asian American and American Indian faculty. Perhaps Asian American faculty have not attracted much attention in the research literature because they are noticeably absent in discussions of minority issues in academia, especially affirmative action. Perhaps also they have been excluded from such discussions because it is often assumed that they are not victims of prejudice and discrimination; that is, they are portrayed as the model minority (Kang, 1996; Lee, 1995; Wu, 1995). On the other hand, American Indians have escaped attention in the research literature on minority faculty because they are *missing* in academia, both as students and faculty. In particular, many American Indian faculty are located in tribal colleges or institutions that serve areas with a large American Indian population (Darden, Bagaka's, Armstrong, and Payne, 1994; Pavel and others, 1998). As a result, American Indian faculty are overlooked if one focuses only on institutions in academia's mainstream.

A need exists for substantive comparisons between minority groups in the faculty population. A research strategy that permits an examination of similarities and differences in the workplace experiences of women and men minority faculty facilitates our understanding of how minority status and gender function as status characteristics in the academic workplace (for interesting discussions and examples, see Calasanti and Smith, 1998; Harris, 1992; Kulis, Ching, and Shaw, 1999; Kupenda, 1997; Niemann, 1999; Turner and Myers, 2000). More important, it would permit one to make observations of general workplace experiences in the minority faculty population. A comparative research strategy would allow one to address the following questions:

1. How do minority groups adapt to the academic workplace? How do they respond to obstacles encountered in the academic workplace? Are there similarities or differences in the manner in which minority groups

adapt and respond to obstacles in the academic workplace?

2. Does each minority group encounter a particular set of obstacles in the academic workplace? Do different obstacles result in competing responses by minority group faculty? What role does the academic culture play in maintaining competing obstacles for minority group faculty?

3. What are the similarities and differences in how minority group faculty negotiate their institutional presence? How does institutional presence vary with minority group membership? That is, do minority groups compete with each other in the academic workplace in the process of negotiating their institutional presence?

The culture of the academic workplace must alter its perception and treatment of women and minority faculty to respond to the changing character of U.S. society. One aspect of the United States's changing character is that women and minorities will be noticeable participants in the workforce of the 21st century, with the result that women and minorities will be a formidable challenge in the workplace. For academia, women and minorities will challenge a faculty culture that rewards White men faculty at the expense of women and minority faculty (see, for example, Aguirre, 1981; Reed, 1986; Buchen, 1992; Josey, 1993; Gonzalez, 1991). It thus rests on us to ask how academia can alter its academic culture to incorporate women and minority faculty as full participants in the academic workplace. The preceding questions for instructing us with regard to the participation of women and minority faculty in the academic workplace can be put into a conceptual framework as follows:

- *The academic culture and diversity:* Institutional initiatives need to be implemented in academia that incorporate diversity in the academic culture as a real-life experience. As such, women and minority faculty, as signals of diversity, become members, rather than peripheral participants, in the academic workplace.
- *Faculty values and diversity:* Institutional initiatives that promote diversity in academia must alter faculty values that are biased against women and minority faculty. By

removing biased faculty values, the academic culture will promote positive perceptions of women and minority faculty.

- *The academic workplace and diversity:* An academic culture that promotes positive perceptions of women and minority faculty will reduce the role conflict they experience in the workplace. A reduction in role conflict will allow women and minority faculty to fully actualize their presence in the workplace, and their faculty work will promote diversity in the workplace.
- *Professional socialization and diversity:* By incorporating diversity in the academic culture and faculty values, the academic workplace will become more responsive to the professional socialization of women and minority faculty. In turn, the responsiveness of the academic workplace to the professional socialization of women and minority faculty will signal the diversification of the academic culture.

REFERENCES

Aguirre, A., Jr. (1981). Chicano faculty in post-secondary educational institutions. *California Journal of Teacher Education, 8,* 11–19.

Aguirre, A., Jr. (1985). Chicano faculty at postsecondary educational institutions in the Southwest. *Journal of Educational Equity and Leadership, 5,* 133–144.

Aguirre, A., Jr. (1987). An interpretative analysis of Chicano faculty in academe. *Social Science Journal, 24,* 71–81.

Aguirre, A., Jr. (1994). *Racism in higher education: A perilous climate for minorities* (IHELG Monograph 93–8). Houston, TX: Institute for Higher Education, Law, and Governance, University of Houston.

Aguirre, A., Jr. (1995a). A Chicano farmworker in academe. In R. Padilla and R. Chavez (Eds.), *The leaning ivory tower: Latino professors in American universities* (pp. 17–27). Albany, NY: SUNY Press.

Aguirre, A., Jr. (1995b). The status of minority faculty in academe. *Equity and Excellence in Education, 28,* 63–68.

Aguirre, A., Jr. (1997, February 21–23). *Affirmative action in academia: A counter-story about exclusion.* Paper presented at the annual meeting of Sociology of Education, Monterey, CA.

Aguirre, A., Jr., Hernandez, A., and Martinez, R. (1994). Perceptions of the workplace: Focus on minority women faculty. *Initiatives, 56,* 41–50.

Aguirre, A., Jr., and Martinez, R. O. (1993). *Chicanos in higher education: Issues and dilemmas for the 21st century.* ASHE-ERIC Higher Education Report No. 3. Washington, DC: The George Washington University, Graduate School of Education and Human Development.

Aguirre, A., Jr., and Turner, J. (1998). *American ethnicity: The dynamics and consequences of discrimination* (2nd ed.). New York: McGraw-Hill.

Allaire, Y., and Firsirotu, M. (1984). Theories of organizational culture. *Organizational Studies, 5,* 193–226.

Allen, W., Epps, E., and Haniff, N. (Eds.). (1991). *College in black and white: African American students in predominantly white and in historically black public universities.* Albany, NY: SUNY Press.

Alpert, D. (1989). Gender inequity in academia: An empirical analysis. *Initiatives, 52,* 9–14.

Arce, C. (1976). Chicanos in higher education. *Integrated Education, 14,* 14–18.

Arce, C. (1978). Chicano participation in academe: A case of academic colonialism. *Grito del Sol: A Chicano Quarterly, 3,* 75–104.

Astin, H., and Bayer, A. (1972). Sex discrimination in academe. *Educational Record, 53,* 101–118.

Astin, H., and Davis, D. (1985). Research productivity across the life and career cycles: Facilitators and barriers for women. In M. Fox (Ed.), *Scholarly writing and publishing: Issues, problems and solutions* (pp. 147–160). Boulder, CO: Westview Press.

Austin, A. (1990). Faculty cultures, faculty values. In W. Tierney (Ed.), *Assessing academic climates and cultures* (pp. 61–74). San Francisco: Jossey-Bass.

Austin, A., and Gamson, Z. (1983). *Academic workplace: New demands, heightened tensions.* ASHE-ERIC Higher Education Research Report No. 10. Washington, DC: Association for the Study of Higher Education.

Ayer, M. (1984). Women, space, and power in higher education. In E. Fennema and M. Ayer (Eds.), *Women and education: Equity or equality?* (pp. 221–238). Berkeley, CA: McCutchan.

Banks, W. (1984). Afro-American scholars in the university. *American Behavioral Scientist, 27,* 325–338.

Barbezat, D. (1987). Salary differentials or sex discrimination? *Population Research and Policy Review, 6,* 69–84.

Bartlett, R. (1997). Report of the committee on the status of women in the economics profession. *American Economic Review, 87,* 506–511.

Bell, D. (1966). *The reforming of general education: The Columbia College experience in its natural setting.* New York: Columbia University Press.

Bell, D. (1986). Strangers in academic paradise: Law teachers of color in still white schools. *University of San Francisco Law Review, 20,* 385–395.

Bell, D. (1987). *And we are not saved: The elusive quest for racial justice.* New York: Basic Books.

Bell, D. (1995). Who's afraid of critical race theory? *University of Illinois Law Review,* 893–910.

Bell, D. (1997a). California's Proposition 209: A temporary diversion on the road to racial disaster. *Loyola of Los Angeles Law Review, 30,* 1447–1464.

Bell, D. (1997b, April 4). Protecting diversity programs from political and judicial attack. *Chronicle of Higher Education,* B4–B5.

Bellas, M. (1997). Disciplinary differences in faculty salaries: Does gender bias play a role? *Journal of Higher Education, 68,* 299–321.

Bellas, M., and Toutkoushian, R. (1999). Faculty time allocations and research productivity: Gender, race, and family effects. *The Review of Higher Education, 22,* 367–390.

Belman, D., and Heywood, J. (1991). Sheepskin effects in the returns to education: An examination of women and minorities. *Review of Economics and Statistics, 73,* 720–724.

Bentley, R., and Blackburn, R. (1992). Two decades of gains for female faculty? *Teachers College Record, 93,* 697–709.

Bernstein, A., and Cock, J. (1994, June 15). A troubling picture of gender equity. *Chronicle of Higher Education,* B1–B3.

Billard, L. (1994). Twenty years later: Is there parity for academic women? *Thought and Action, 10,* 115–144.

Blackburn, R., and Lawrence, J. (1995). *Faculty at work: Motivation, expectation, satisfaction.* Baltimore: Johns Hopkins University Press.

Blackwell, J. (1989, September/October). Mentoring: An action strategy for increasing minority faculty. *Academe,* 8–14.

Bloom, A. (1987). *The closing of the American mind.* New York: Simon and Schuster.

Bogart, K. (1985). Improving sex equity in postsecondary education. In S. Klein (Ed.), *Handbook for achieving sex equity through education* (pp. 470–488). Baltimore: Johns Hopkins University Press.

Bognanno, M. (1987). Women in professions: Academic women. In K. Koziora, M. Mokow, and L. Tanner (Eds.), *Working women, past, present, and future* (pp. 245–264). Washington, DC: Bureau of National Affairs.

Brasskamp, L. (1978). Determining salary equity: Policies, procedures, and problems. *Journal of Higher Education, 49,* 231–246.

Brinson, J., and Kottler, J. (1993). Cross-cultural mentoring in counselor education: A strategy for retaining minority faculty. *Counselor Education and Supervision, 32,* 241–253.

Brodie, J., and Wiley, E. (1990). The campus-wide trauma of discrimination litigation. *Black Issues in Higher Education, 7, 1,* 26–27.

Bromberg, M. (1993). Harvard Law School's war over faculty diversity. *Journal of Blacks in Higher Education, 1,* 75–82.

Bronstein, P. (1993). Challenges, rewards, and costs for feminist and ethnic minority scholars. In J. Gainen and R. Boice (Eds.), *Building a diverse faculty* (pp. 61–70). New Directions for Teaching and Research No. 53. San Francisco: Jossey-Bass.

Brooks, R. (1982). Affirmative action in law teaching. *Columbia Human Rights Law Review, 14,* 15–48.

Brown, D. (1990). Racism and race relations in the university. *Virginia Law Review, 76,* 295–335.

Buchen, I. (1992). The impact of cultural diversity on faculty and students. *Equity and Excellence, 25,* 228–232.

Bunzel, J. (1990). Minority faculty hiring: Problems and prospects. *American Scholar, 59,* 39–52.

Burns, M. (1993). Service courses: Doing women a disservice. *Academe, 79,* 18–21.

Cadet, N. (1989). Marginalia: Women in the academic workplace. *Feminist Teacher, 4,* 16–18.

Calasanti, T., and Smith, J. (1998). A critical evaluation of the experiences of women and minority faculty: Some implications for occupational research. *Current Research on Occupations and Professions, 10,* 239–258.

Carroll, C. (1973). Three's a crowd: The dilemma of the black woman in higher education. In A. Rossi (Ed.), *Academic women on the move* (pp. 173–185). New York: Russell Sage.

Carter, D., and O'Brien, E. (1993). *Employment and hiring patterns for faculty of color.* Washington, DC: American Council on Education.

Carter, H. (1982). *Making it in academia: Gurus can get you there.* (ED 235 758).

Chaffee, E., and Tierney, W. (1988). *Collegiate culture and leadership strategies.* New York: American Council on Education/Macmillan.

Chamberlain, M. (1988). *Women in academe: Progress and prospects.* New York: Russell Sage.

Chatman, J. (1989). Improving interactional organizational research: A model of person-organization fit. *Academy of Management Review, 14,* 333–349.

Chepyator-Thomson, J., and King, S. (1996). Scholarship reconsidered: Considerations for a more inclusive scholarship in the academy. *Quest, 48,* 165–174.

Chew, P. (1996). Asian Americans in the legal academy: An empirical and narrative profile. *Asian Law Journal, 3,* 7–38.

Chused, R. (1988). The hiring and retention of minorities and women in American law school faculties. *University of Pennsylvania Law Review, 137,* 537–569.

Clark, B. (1970). *The distinctive college.* Chicago: Aldine.

Clark, B. (1972). The organizational saga in higher education. *Administrative Science Quarterly, 17,* 179–194.

Clark, B. (1984). *The higher education system: Academic organization in cross-national perspective.* Berkeley, CA: University of California Press.

Clark, B. (1985). Listening to the professorate. *Change, 17,* 36–43.

Clark, S., and Corcoran, M. (1986). Perspective on the professional socialization of women faculty: A case of accumulative disadvantage. *Journal of Higher Education, 57,* 20–43.

Cohen, A. (1974). Community college faculty job satisfaction. *Research in Higher Education, 2,* 369–376.

Contreras, A. R. (1995). The odyssey of a Chicano academic. In R. Padilla and R. Chavez (Eds.), *The leaning ivory tower: Latino professors in American universities* (pp. 111–129). Albany, NY: SUNY Press.

Contreras, A. R. (1998). Leading from the margins in the ivory tower. In L. Valverde and L. Castenell (Eds.), *The multicultural campus: Strategies for transforming higher education* (pp. 137–166). Walnut Creek, CA: AltaMira Press.

Conway, J. (1989). Higher education for women: Models for the twenty-first century. *American Behavioral Scientist, 32,* 633–639.

Copeland, J., and Murray, J. (1996). Getting tossed from the ivory tower: The legal implications of evaluating faculty performance. *Missouri Law Review, 61,* 233–327.

Cortese, A. (1992). Affirmative action: Are white women gaining at the expense of black men? *Equity and Excellence in Education, 25,* 77–99.

Cox, T. (1991). The multicultural organization. *Academy of Management Executive, 5,* 34–47.

Cox, T., and Nkomo, S. (1990). Invisible men and women: A status report on race as a variable in organization behavior research. *Journal of Organizational Behavior, 11,* 419–431.

Creamer, E. (1998). *Assessing faculty publication productivity: Issues of equity.* ASHE-ERIC Higher Education Report (Vol. 26, No. 2). Washington, DC: The George Washington University, Graduate School of Education and Human Development.

Culp, J. (1992). Posner on Duncan Kennedy and racial difference: White authority in the legal academy. *Duke Law Journal, 1992,* 1095–1113.

Darden, J., Bagaka's, J., Armstrong, T., and Payne, T. (1994). Segregation of American Indian undergraduate students in institutions of higher education. *Equity and Excellence in Education, 27,* 61–68.

Davis, L. (1985). Black and white social work faculty: Perceptions of respect, satisfaction, and job permanence. *Journal of Sociology and Social Welfare, 12,* 79–94.

Dejoie, C. (1977). The black women in alienation in white academia. *Negro Educational Review, 28,* 4–12.

Delgado, R. (1988). *Minority law professors' lives: The Bell-Delgado survey.* Madison, WI: University of Wisconsin-Madison Law School, Institute of Legal Studies.

Delgado, R. (1991). Affirmative action as a majoritarian device, or, Do you really want to be a role model? *Michigan Law Review, 89,* 1222–1231.

de los Santos, A. (1994). Minority faculty recruitment and retention strategies: The Maricopa experience. *New Directions for Community Colleges, 22,* 73–80.

Denton, M., and Zeytinoglu, U. (1993). Perceived participation in decision-making in a university setting: The impact of gender. *Industrial and Labor Relations Review, 46,* 320–331.

Dey, E. (1994). Dimensions of faculty stress: A recent survey. *Review of Higher Education, 17,* 305–322.

Dickey, C. (1996). *Mentoring women of color at the University of Minnesota: Challenges for organizational transformation.* (ED 399 838).

Dill, D. (1982). The management of academic culture: Notes on the management of meaning and social integration. *Higher Education, 11,* 303–320.

DiNitto, D., Aguilar, M., Franklin, C., and Jordan, C. (1995). Over the edge? Women and tenure in today's academic environment. *Affilia, 10,* 255–279.

D'Souza, D. (1991). *Illiberal education: The politics of race and sex on campus.* New York: Free Press.

Edgert, P. (1994). Assessing campus climate: Implications for diversity. In D. Smith, L. Wolf, and T. Levitan (Eds.), *Studying diversity in higher education* (pp. 51–62). San Francisco: Jossey-Bass.

Elmore, C., and Blackburn, R. (1983). Black and white faculty in white research universities. *Journal of Higher Education, 54,* 1–15.

Epps, E. (1989). Academic culture and the minority professor. *Academe, 36,* 23–26.

Ervin, D., Thomas, B., and Zey-Ferrell, M. (1984). Sex discrimination and rewards in a public comprehensive university. *Human Relations, 37,* 1005–1025.

Everett, K., DeLoach, W., and Bressan, S. (1996). Women in the ranks: Faculty trends in the ACS-approved departments. *Journal of Chemical Education, 73,* 139–141.

Exum, W. (1983). Climbing the crystal stair: Values, affirmative action, and minority faculty. *Social Problems, 30,* 383–399.

Exum, W., Menges, R., Watkins, B., and Berglund, P. (1984). Making it at the top: Women and minority faculty in the academic labor market. *American Behavioral Scientist, 27,* 301–324.

Ezrati, J. (1983). Personnel policies in higher education: A covert means of sex discrimination? *Educational Administration Quarterly, 19,* 105–119.

Feagin, J., Vera, H., and Imani, N. (1996). *The agony of education: Black students at white colleges and universities.* New York: Routledge.

Feild, H., and Giles, W. (1977). Dimensions of faculty members' sensitivity to job satisfaction items. *Research in Higher Education, 6,* 193–199.

Fields, C. (1988, May 11). Hispanics, state's fastest-growing minority, shut out of top positions at U. of California, leaders say. *Chronicle of Higher Education,* A9–A10.

Fields, C. (1996). A morale dilemma. *Black Issues in Higher Education, 13,* 22–23, 25–26, 28–29.

Finkel, S., and Olswang, S. (1994, November). *Impediments to tenure for female assistant professors.* Paper presented at the annual meeting of the Association for the Study of Higher Education, Tucson, AZ.

Finkel, S., and Olswang, S. (1996). Child rearing as a career impediment to women assistant professors. *Review of Higher Education, 19,* 123–139.

Finkel, S., Olswang, S., and She, N. (1994). Childbirth, tenure, and promotion for women faculty. *Review of Higher Education, 17,* 259–270.

Finkelstein, M. (1978). *Three decades of research on American academics: A descriptive portrait and synthesis of findings.* Ph.D. dissertation, SUNY–Buffalo.

Finkelstein, M. (1982). *Women and minority faculty: A synthesis of extant researchers.* (ED 219 015).

Finkelstein, M. (1984). The status of academic women: An assessment of five competing explanations. *Review of Higher Education, 7,* 223–246.

Fontaine, D., and Greenlee, S. (1993). Black women: Double solos in the workplace. *Western Journal of Black Studies, 17,* 121–125.

Ford, D. (1984). *Faculty salary differentials by race: A management school case study of suspected treatment discrimination.* (ED 265 753).

Freeman, R. (1977a). Faculty women in the American universities: Up the down staircase. *Higher Education, 6,* 165–188.

Freeman, R. (1977b). The new job market for black academicians. *Industrial and Labor Relations Review, 30,* 161–174.

Gallant, M., and Cross, J. (1993). Wayward Puritans in the ivory tower: Collective aspects of gender discrimination in academia. *Sociological Quarterly, 34,* 237–256.

Garcia, E. (1978). Joint faculty appointments: An administrative dilemma in Chicano studies. *Exploration in Ethnic Studies, 2,* 1–8.

Garza, H. (1988). The "barrioization" of Hispanic faculty. *Educational Record, 69,* 122–124.

Gmelch, W., Lovrich, N., and Wilke, P. (1984). Stress in academe: A national perspective. *Research in Higher Education, 20,* 477–490.

Gmelch, W., Wilke, P., and Lovrich, N. (1986). Dimensions of stress among university faculty: Factor-analytic results from a national study. *Research in Higher Education, 24,* 266–286.

Golbe, D. (1985). Imperfect signaling, affirmative action and black-white wage differentials. *Southern Economic Journal, 51,* 842–848.

Gonzales, A. (1991). Facilitating cultural diversity: A Latino perspective. *ACA Bulletin, 78,* 46–49.

Gose, B. (1996, May 24). Minority students were 24% of college enrollment in 1994. *Chronicle of Higher Education,* A32.

Gose, B. (1998, September 18). A sweeping new defense of affirmative action. *Chronicle of Higher Education,* A46–A48.

Grandbois, G., Andrews, S., and Schadt, D. (1996). Minority faculty's perceptions of selected workplace conditions. *Perceptual and Motor Skills, 82,* 648–650.

Granger, M. (1993). A review of the literature on the status of women and minorities in the professorate in higher education. *Journal of School Leadership, 3,* 121–135.

Gray, M. (1985). The halls of ivy and the halls of justice: Resisting sex discrimination against faculty women. *Academe, 71,* 33–41.

Greene, L. (1991). Serving the community: Aspiration and abyss for the law professor of color. *Saint Louis University Public Law Review, 10,* 297–303.

Grillo, T. (1997). Tenure and minority women law professors: Separating the strands. *University of San Francisco Law Review, 31,* 747–755.

Grunig, L. (1989). Sex discrimination in promotion and tenure in journalism education. *Journalism Quarterly, 66,* 93–100.

Gummer, B. (1998). Current perspectives on diversity in the workforce: How diverse is diverse? *Administration in Social Work, 22,* 83–101.

Hagedorn, L. (1995, November 2–5). *Wage equity and female faculty job satisfaction: The role of wage differentials in a job satisfaction causal model.* Paper presented at the annual meeting of the Association for the Study of Higher Education, Orlando, FL.

Haines, A. (1991). Reflections on minority law professors balancing their duties and their personal commitments to community service and academic duties. *Saint Louis University Public Law Review, 10,* 305–323.

Haney-Lopez, I. (1991). Community ties, race, and faculty hiring: The case for professors who don't think white. *Reconstruction, 1,* 46–62.

Hanson, D. (1995). Funding for RAND is frozen in Clinton's 1996 budget proposal. *Chemical and Engineering News, 73,* 18–26.

Harris, C. (1992). Law professors of color and the academy: Of poets and kings. *Chicago-Kent Law Review, 68,* 331–352.

Hayes, M. (1990, April). *Minority women in higher education: Status and challenges.* Paper presented at the annual meeting of the Comparative and International Educational Society, Anaheim, CA.

Heilman, M. (1994). Affirmative action: Some unintended consequences for working women. In B. Staw and L. Cummings (Eds.), *Research in organizational behavior, Vol. 16* (pp. 125–169). Greenwich, CT: JAI Press.

Henry, M. (1990). Voices of academic women on feminine gender scripts. *British Journal of Sociology of Education, 11,* 121–135.

Henry, W., and Nixon, H. (1994). Changing a campus climate for minorities and women. *Equity and Excellence in Education, 27,* 48–55.

Hensel, N. (1991). *Realizing gender equality in higher education: The need to integrate work/family issues.* ASHE-ERIC Higher Education Report No. 2. Washington, DC: The George Washington University, Graduate School of Education and Human Development.

Hewlett, S. (1986). *A lesser life: The myth of women's liberation in America.* New York: William Morrow.

Higgerson, M., and Higgerson, R. (1991). Affirmative action guidelines: Do they impede progress? *CUPA Journal, 42*(4), 11–14.

Hill, M. (1986–87). A theoretical analysis of faculty job satisfaction/dissatisfaction. *Educational Research Quarterly, 10,* 36–44.

Hirano-Nakanishi, M. (1994). Methodological issues in the study of diversity in higher education. In D. Smith, L. Wolf, and T. Levitan (Eds.), *Studying diversity in higher education* (pp. 63–85). San Francisco: Jossey-Bass.

Hofstede, G. (1980). *Culture's consequence.* Beverly Hills, CA: Sage.

Hollon, C., and Gemmill, G. (1976). A comparison of female and male professors on participation in decision-making, job-related tension, job involvement, and job satisfaction. *Educational Administration Quarterly, 12,* 80–93.

Hu-DeHart, E. (1983). Women, minorities, and academic freedom. In C. Kaplan and E. Schrecker (Eds.), *Regulating the intellectuals: Perspectives in academic freedom in the 1980s* (pp. 141–159). New York: Praeger.

Hughes, J. (1998). Reverse discrimination and higher education faculty. *Michigan Journal of Race & Law, 3,* 395–415.

Ibarra, H. (1993). Personal networks of women and minorities in management: A conceptual framework. *Academy of Management Review, 18,* 56–87.

Ibarra, H. (1995). Race, opportunity, and diversity of social circles in managerial networks. *Academy of Management Journal, 38,* 673–703.

Institute for the Study of Student Change. (1990). *The diversity project: An interim report to the chancellor.* Berkeley, CA: University of California, Office of the Chancellor.

Irvine, J., and Walker, V. (1998, April 30). Treatment does not confer status. *Black Issues in Higher Education,* 72.

Jackson, C. (1996). *African-American women's mentoring experiences.* (ED 401 371).

Jackson, K. (1991). Black faculty in academia. In P. Altbach and K. Lomotey (Eds.), *The racial crisis in American higher education* (pp. 135–148). Albany, NY: SUNY Press.

Jarrell, R. (1952). *Pictures from an institution.* New York: Avon Books.

Jencks, C., and Riesman, D. (1968). *The academic revolution.* New York: Doubleday.

Jevons, M. (1985). *The fatal equilibrium.* New York: Ballantine.

Johnsrud, L. (1993). Women and minority faculty experiences: Defining and responding to diverse realities. *New Directions for Teaching and Learning, 53,* 3–16.

Johnsrud, L., and Des Jarlais, C. (1994). Barriers to tenure for women and minorities. *Review of Higher Education, 17,* 335–353.

Johnsrud, L., and Sadao, K. (1998). The common experience of "otherness": Ethnic and racial minority faculty. *Review of Higher Education, 21,* 315–342.

Johnsrud, L., and Wunsch, M. (1991). Junior and senior faculty women: Commonalities and differences in perceptions of academic life. *Psychological Reports, 69,* 879–886.

Johnston, W. (1987). *Workforce 2000: Work and workers for the 21st century.* Indianapolis, IN: Hudson Institute.

Jordan, K. (1998). Diversity training in the workplace today: A status report. *Journal of Career Planning and Employment, 58,* 46–56.

Josey, E. (1993). The challenges of cultural diversity in the recruitment of faculty and students from diverse backgrounds. *Journal of Education for Library and Information Science, 34,* 302–311.

Justus, J. (1987). *The University of California in the twenty-first century: Successful approaches to faculty diversity.* (ED 379 987).

Kang, J. (1996). Negative action against Asian Americans: The internal instability of Dworkin's defense of affirmative action. *Harvard Civil Rights–Civil Liberties Law Review, 31,* 1–47.

Kanter, R. (1977). Some effects of proportions on group life: Skewed sex ratios and responses to token women. *American Journal of Sociology, 82,* 965–990.

Kanter, R. (1980). Quality of work life and work behavior in academia. *National Forum, 60,* 35–38.

Keller, G. (1983). *Academic strategy: The management revolution in American higher education.* Baltimore: Johns Hopkins University Press.

Kelly, J. (1989). Gender, pay and job satisfaction in journalism. *Journalism Quarterly, 66,* 446–452.

Kerr, C. (1997). Speculations about the increasingly indeterminate future of higher education in the United States. *Review of Higher Education, 20,* 345–356.

Kimball, R. (1990). *Tenured radicals: How politics has corrupted our higher education.* New York: Harper Perennial.

Kuh, G., and Whitt, E. (1988). *The invisible tapestry: Culture in American colleges and universities.* ASHE-ERIC Higher Education Report No. 1. Washington, DC: Association for the Study of Higher Education.

Kulis, S., Ching, Y., and Shaw, H. (1999). Discriminatory organizational contexts and black scientists on postsecondary faculties. *Research in Higher Education, 40,* 115–148.

Kupenda, A. (1997). Making traditional courses more inclusive: Confessions of an African American female professor who attempted to crash all the barriers at once. *University of San Francisco Law Review, 31,* 975–992.

La Belle, T., and Ward, C. (1996). *Ethnic studies and multiculturalism.* Albany, NY: SUNY Press.

Larwood, L., Gutek, B., and Gattiker, U. (1984). Perspective on institutional discrimination and resistance to change. *Group and Organization Studies, 9,* 333–352.

Lawler, A. (1995). Scientists mobilize to fight cuts. *Science, 268,* 1120–1122.

Lee, C. (1995). Beyond black and white: Racializing Asian Americans in a society obsessed with O.J. *Hasting's Women's Law Journal, 6,* 165–207.

Levine, A. (1991). Editorial. The meaning of diversity. *Change, 23,* 4–5.

Locke, E., Fitzpatrick, W., and White, F. (1983). Job satisfaction and role clarity among university and college faculty. *Review of Higher Education, 6,* 343–365.

Luna, G. (1990). Understanding gender-based wage discrimination: Legal interpretation and trends of pay equity in higher education. *Journal of Law and Education, 19,* 371–384.

Luna, G., and Cullen, D. L. (1995). *Empowering the faculty: Mentoring redirected and renewed.* ASHE-ERIC Higher Education Report No. 3. Washington, DC: The George Washington University, Graduate School of Education and Human Development. (ED 399 889).

Macilwain, C. (1997). Real fall in U.S. research funding revealed. *Nature, 385,* 283.

Magner, D. (1997, November 21). The number of minority Ph.D.'s reached an all-time high in 1996. *Chronicle of Higher Education,* A10–A11.

Malveaux, J. (1996, October 17). The affirmative action debate and collegiality. *Black Issues in Higher Education,* 41.

Mangan, K. (1994, October 5). Hahnemann U. angers faculty with threat to fire those who don't attract grant money. *Chronicle of Higher Education,* A20.

Mangan, K. (1999, March 12). Stanford law school faces tensions over issues of race and gender. *Chronicle of Higher Education,* A12.

Margolis, E., and Romero, M. (1998). The department is very male, very white, very old, and very conservative: The functioning of the hidden curriculum in graduate sociology departments. *Harvard Educational Review, 68,* 1–32.

Martinez, R., Hernandez, A., and Aguirre, A., Jr. (1993). Latino faculty attitudes toward the workplace. *AMAE Journal,* 45–52.

Matthews, C. (1990). *Underrepresented minorities and women in science, mathematics, and engineering: Problems and issues for the 1990s.* Washington, DC: Congressional Research Service.

Maxson, J., and Hair, B. (1990). *Managing diversity: A key to building a quality work force.* Research and Development Series No. 271. Columbus, OH: Ohio State University Center on Education and Training for Employment.

Mazingo, S. (1987). More efforts needed to retain, promote minority faculty. *Journalism Educator, 41,* 34–36.

McCarthy, M. (1951). *The groves of academe.* New York: Harvest/HBJ Books.

McCombs, H. (1989). The dynamics and impact of affirmative action processes on higher education, the curriculum, and black women. *Sex Roles, 21,* 127–144.

McCormick, T. (1991). *An analysis of some pitfalls of traditional mentoring for minorities and women in higher education.* (ED 334 905).

McKay, N. (1995). Minority faculty in [mainstream white] academia. In A. L. DeNeef and C. Goodwin (Eds.), *The academic's handbook* (2nd ed.), (pp. 49–61). Durham, NC: Duke University Press.

McMillen, L. (1986, December 3). Women's groups: Going the old boys' network one better. *Chronicle of Higher Education,* A15–A17.

McMillen, L. (1987, February 4). Job-related tension and anxiety taking a toll among employees in academe's stress factories. *Chronicle of Higher Education,* A1, A10–A12.

McNeer, E. (1983). Two opportunities for mentoring: A study of women's career development in higher education administration. *Journal of the National Association of Women Deans and Counselors, 47,* 8–14.

Menges, R., and Exum, W. (1983). Barriers to the progress of women and minority faculty. *Journal of Higher Education, 54,* 123–144.

Merritt, D., and Reskin, B. (1992). Sex, race, and credentials: The truth about affirmative action in law faculty hiring. *Columbia Law Review,* 97, 199–300.

Meyer, J., Boli, J., and Thomas, G. (1994). Ontology and rationalization in the western cultural account. In W. R. Scott, J. Meyer, and Associates (Eds.), *Institutional environments and organizations: Structural complexity and individualism* (pp. 9–27). Thousand Oaks, CA: Sage.

Milem, J., and Astin, H. (1993). The changing composition of the faculty: What does it really mean for diversity? *Change, 25,* 21–27.

Milliken, F., and Martins, L. (1996). Searching for common threads: Understanding the multiple effects of diversity in organizational groups. *Academy of Management Review, 21,* 402–433.

Mindiola, T. (1995). Getting tenure at the U. In R. Padilla and R. Chavez (Eds.), *The leaning ivory tower: Latino professors in American universities* (pp. 29–51). Albany, NY: SUNY Press.

Montero-Sieburth, M. (1996). An inquiry into the experience of Latinas in academia. *New England Journal of Public Policy, 11,* 65–97.

Mooney, C. (1988, January 20). The faculty work climate seems more positive to administrators than to professors themselves. *Chronicle of Higher Education,* A11–A12.

Moore, K. (1982). Towards a synthesis of organizational theory and historical analysis: The case of academic women. *Review of Higher Education, 5,* 233–243.

Moore, W. (1987–88). Black faculty in white colleges: A dream deferred. *Educational Record, 69,* 116–121.

Moran, R. (1986). Commentary. The implications of being a society of one. *University of San Francisco Law Review, 20,* 503–513.

Morgan, J. (1996, October 3). Reaching out to young black men: A dedicated and determined group of scholars offer the lure of the academy. *Black Issues in Higher Education,* 16–19.

Mortimer, K., and McConnell, T. (1978). *Sharing authority effectively: Participation, interaction, and discretion.* San Francisco: Jossey-Bass.

Moses, Y. (1997, December 12). Salaries in academe: The gender gap persists. *Chronicle of Higher Education,* A60.

Moy, M. (1995). Asian American education: Better or worse in the 21st century? A look at one state. In G. Thomas (Ed.), *Race and ethnicity in America: Meeting the challenge of the 21st century* (pp. 49–62). Washington, DC: Taylor and Frances.

Myers, S., and Wilkins, R. (1995). *MHEC minority faculty development project.* Minneapolis, MN: Midwestern Higher Education Commission.

Nakanishi, D. (1988). Asian Pacific Americans and selective undergraduate admissions. *Journal of College Admissions, 118,* 17–26.

Nakanishi, D. (1993). Asian Pacific Americans in higher education: Faculty and administrative representation and tenure. *New Directions for Teaching and Learning, 53,* 51–59.

National Center for Education Statistics. (1986). *Digest of education statistics 1985–1986.* Washington, DC: NCES.

National Center for Education Statistics. (1996). *Digest of education statistics 1996.* Washington, DC: NCES.

Nettles, M., and Perna, L. (1995, November 2–5). *Sex and race differences in faculty salaries, tenure, rank, and productivity: Why, on average, do women, African Americans, and Hispanics have lower salaries, tenure, and rank?* Paper presented at the annual meeting of the Association for the Study of Higher Education, Orlando, FL.

Nichols, I., and Golden, M. (1982). *The middle way: Patron as guide*. (ED 235 759).

Niemann, Y. (1999). The making of a token: A case study of stereotype threat, stigma, racism, and tokenism in academia. *Frontiers, 20,* 111–126.

Niemann, Y., and Dovidio, J. (1998). Relationship of solo status, academic rank, and perceived distinctiveness to job satisfaction of racial/ethnic minorities. *Journal of Applied Psychology, 83,* 55–71.

Nieves-Squires, S. (1992). Hispanic women in the U.S. academic context. In L. Welch (Ed.), *Perspectives on minority women in higher education* (pp. 71–92). New York: Praeger.

Nkomo, S. (1992). The emperor has no clothes: Revisiting "Race in organizations." *Academy of Management Review, 17,* 487–513.

Norman, K., and Norman, J. (1995). The synergy of minority student persistence and faculty renewal. *Innovative Higher Education, 20,* 129–140.

Olivas, M. (1988). Latino faculty at the border. *Change, 2,* 6–9.

Olsen, D., Maple, S., and Stage, F. (1995). Women and minority faculty job satisfaction. *Journal of Higher Education, 66,* 267–293.

Ortiz, F. (1998). Career patterns of people of color in academia. In L. Valverde and L. Castenell (Eds.), *The multicultural campus: Strategies for transforming higher education* (pp. 121–135). Walnut Creek, CA: AltaMira Press.

Ottinger, C., and Sikula, R. (1993). *Women in higher education: Where do we stand?* Washington, DC: American Council on Education.

Park, S. (1996). Research, teaching, and service: Why shouldn't women's work count? *Journal of Higher Education, 67,* 47–84.

Parson, L., Sands, R., and Duane, J. (1991). The campus climate for women faculty at a public university. *Initiatives, 54,* 19–27.

Patton, J. (1988). *Black men: Missing in higher education.* Working Paper No. 10. Chicago: University of Chicago Metropolitan Opportunity Project.

Pavel, D. M., Skinner, R., Cahalan, M., Tippiconnic, J., and Stein, W. (1998). *American Indians and Alaska Natives in postsecondary education.* Washington, DC: U.S. Department of Education, Office of Educational Research and Improvement.

Pearson, D., and Seiler, R. (1983). Environmental satisfiers in academe. *Higher Education, 12,* 35–47.

Peterson, M., Cameron, K., Jones, P., Meta, L., and Ettington, D. (1986). *The organizational context for teaching and learning:*

A review of the research literature. Ann Arbor, MI: University of Michigan National Center for Research to Improve Postsecondary Teaching and Learning.

Peterson, M., and Spencer, M. (1990). Understanding academic culture and climate. In W. Tierney (Ed.), *Assessing academic climates and cultures* (pp. 3–18). San Francisco: Jossey-Bass.

Peterson, M., and White, T. (1992). Faculty and administrator perceptions of their environments: Different views or different models of organization? *Research in Higher Education, 33,* 177–204.

Pfeffer, J., and Langton, N. (1993). The effect of wage dispersion on satisfaction, productivity, and working collaboratively: Evidence from college and university faculty. *Administrative Science Quarterly, 38,* 382–407.

Phelps, R. (1995). What's in a number? Implications for African American female faculty at predominantly white colleges and universities. *Innovative Higher Education, 19,* 255–268.

Phillips, M.-C. (1993). Tenure trap: Number of obstacles stand in way of tenure for women. *Black Issues In Higher Education, 10,* 42–44.

Plata, M. (1996). Retaining ethnic minority faculty at institutions of higher education. *Journal of Instructional Psychology, 23,* 221–227.

Plater, W. (1995). Future work: Faculty time in the 21st century. *Change, 27,* 22–34.

Pounder, D. (1989). The gender gap in salaries of educational administration professors. *Educational Administration Quarterly, 25,* 181–201.

Powell, M. (1998). Campus climate and students of color. In L. Valverde and L. Castenell (Eds.), *The multicultural campus: Strategies for transforming higher education* (pp. 95–118). Walnut Creek, CA: AltaMira Press.

Ransom, M., and Megdal, S. (1993). Sex differences in the academic labor market in the affirmative action era. *Economics of Education Review, 12,* 21–43.

Rausch, D., Ortiz, B., Douthitt, R., and Reed, L. (1989). The academic revolving door: Why do women get caught? *CUPA Journal, 40,* 1–16.

Reed, R. (1986). Faculty diversity: An educational and moral imperative in search of institutional commitment. *Journal of Educational Equity and Leadership, 6,* 274–294.

Reyes, M., and Halcon, J. (1988). Racism in academia: The old wolf revisited. *Harvard Educational Review, 58,* 299–314.

Reyes, M., and Halcon, J. (1991). Practices of the academy: Barriers to access to Chicano academics. In P. Altbach and K. Lomotey (Eds.), *The racial crisis in American higher education* (pp. 167–186). Albany, NY: SUNY Press.

Rice, R. (1986). The academic profession in transition: Toward a new social fiction. *Teaching Sociology, 14,* 12–23.

Rich, H., and Jolicoeur, P. (1978). Faculty role perceptions and preferences in the seventies. *Sociology of Work and Occupations, 5,* 423–445.

Rickard, S. (1993). Truth, freedom, justice: Academic tradition and the essential values. *New Directions for Student Services, 61,* 15–23.

Riger, S., Stokes, J., Raja, S., and Sullivan, M. (1997). Measuring perceptions of the work environment for female faculty. *Review of Higher Education, 21,* 63–78.

Roberts, D. (1993). Community: The value of social synergy. *New Directions for Student Services, 61,* 35–45.

Robin, H., and Robin, S. (1983). Women's salaries in higher education: A case study. *Journal of Educational Equity and Leadership, 3,* 39–56.

Rodriguez, G., and Takaki, R. (1998, October 5). California's big squeeze. *Nation,* 21–23.

Rosenblum, G., and Rosenblum, B. (1990). Segmented labor markets in institutions of higher learning. *Sociology of Education, 63,* 151–164.

Russell, J. (1995). On being a gorilla in your midst, or, The life of one black woman in the legal academy. In R. Delgado (Ed.), *Critical race theory: The cutting edge* (pp. 498–501). Philadelphia: Temple University Press.

Russell, S. (1991). The status of women and minorities in higher education: Findings from the 1988 National Survey of Postsecondary Faculty. *CUPA Journal, 42,* 1–11.

Sanders, K., and Mellow, G. (1990). Permanent diversity: The deferred vision of higher education. *Initiatives, 53,* 9–13.

Sandler, B., and Hall, R. (1986). *The campus climate revisited: Chilly for women faculty, administrators, and graduate students.* Washington, DC: Project on the Status and Education of Women, Association of American Colleges.

Sands, R., Parson, L. A., and Duane, J. (1992). Faculty-faculty mentoring and discrimination: Perceptions among Asian, Asian American, and Pacific Island faculty. *Equity and Excellence, 25,* 124–129.

Scheff, T. (1995). Academic gangs. *Crime, Law and Social Change, 23,* 157–162.

Schiele, J. (1992). Disparities between African-American women and men on social work faculty. *Affilia, 7,* 44–56.

Schneider, A. (1997, June 20). Proportion of minority professors inches up to about 10%. *Chronicle of Higher Education,* A12–A13.

Schneider, A. (1998, November 20). What has happened to faculty diversity in California? *Chronicle of Higher Education,* A10–A12.

Schomberg, S., and Farmer, J. (1994). The evolving concept of public service and implications for rewarding faculty. *Continuing Higher Education Review, 58,* 122–140.

Seidman, E. (1983, April). *The few among the many: Interviews of minority college faculty.* Paper presented at the annual meeting of the American Educational Research Association, Montreal, PQ.

Shavlik, D., Touchton, J., and Pearson, C. (1989). The new agenda of women in higher education. In C. Pearson, D. Shavlik, and J. Touchton (Eds.), *Educating the majority: Women challenge tradition in higher education* (pp. 441–458). New York: Macmillan.

Shropshire, K. (1996). Merit, ol' boy networks, and the black-bottomed pyramid. *Hastings Law Journal, 47,* 455–472.

Simeone, A. (1987). *Academic women: Working toward equality.* Boston: Bergin and Garvey.

Singh, K., Robinson, A., and Williams-Green, J. (1995). Difference in perceptions of African American women and men faculty and administrators. *Journal of Negro Education, 64,* 401–408.

Smart, J. (1978). Diversity of academic organizations: Faculty incentives. *Journal of Higher Education, 49,* 403–419.

Smith, C., and Hixson, V. (1987). The work of the university professor: Evidence of segmented labor markets inside the academy. *Current Research on Occupations and Professions, 4,* 159–180.

Smith, D. (1996). *The pipeline for achieving faculty diversity: Debunking the myths.* (ED 402 836).

Smith, E., Anderson, J., and Lovrich, N. (1995). The multiple sources of workplace stress among land-grant university faculty. *Research in Higher Education, 36,* 261–282.

Smith, P. (1990). *Killing the spirit: Higher education in America.* New York: Viking.

Sowers-Hoag, K., and Harrison, D. (1991). Women in social work education: Progress or promise? *Journal of Social Work Education, 27,* 320–328.

Stassen, M. (1995). White faculty members and racial diversity: A theory and its implications. *Review of Higher Education, 18,* 361–391.

Stecklein, J., and Lorenz, G. (1986). Academic women: Twenty-four years of progress? *Liberal Education, 72,* 63–71.

Steers, R. (1991). *Introduction to organizational behavior.*
New York: Harper Collins.

Steward, R., Patterson, B., Morales, P., Bartell, P., Dinas, P., and
Powers, R. (1995). Women in higher education and job satisfaction: Does interpersonal style matter? *NASPA Journal, 33,* 45–53.

Stewart, P. (1995). The academic community. In A. L. DeNeef and
C. D. Goodwin (Eds.), *The academic's handbook* (2nd ed.),
(pp. 334–340). Durham, NC: Duke University Press.

Sykes, C. (1988). *ProfScam: Professors and the demise of higher
education.* New York: St. Martin's Press.

Tack, M. W., and Patitu, C. L. (1992). *Faculty job satisfaction:
Women and minorities in peril.* ASHE-ERIC Higher Education
Report No. 4. Washington, DC: The George Washington
University, Graduate School of Education and Human
Development.

Takagi, D. 1994. Post–Civil Rights politics and Asian-American
identity: Admissions and higher education. In S. Gregory and
R. Sonjek (Eds.), Race (pp. 229–242). New Brunswick, NJ:
Rutgers University Press.

Thomas, G., and Asunka, K. (1995). Employment and quality of life
of minority and women faculty in a predominantly white institution. In G. Thomas (Ed.), *Race and ethnicity in America:
Meeting the challenge in the 21st century* (pp. 295–308).
Washington, DC: Taylor and Francis.

Tierney, W. (1988). Organizational culture in higher education.
Journal of Higher Education, 59, 2–21.

Tierney, W., and Bensimon, E. (1996). *Promotion and tenure:
Community and socialization in academe.* Albany, NY:
SUNY Press.

Toth, E. (1995). Women in academia. In A. DeNeef and C.
Goodwin (Eds.), *The academic's handbook* (2nd ed.),
(pp. 38–47). Durham, NC: Duke University Press.

Toutkoushian, R. (1998). Racial and marital status differences in
faculty pay. *Journal of Higher Education, 69,* 513–541.

Turner, C., and Myers, S., Jr. (2000). *Faculty of color in academe:
Bittersweet success.* Boston: Allyn and Bacon.

Valverde, L. (1998). Future strategies and actions: Creating
multicultural higher education campuses. In L. Valverde and
L. Castenell (Eds.), *The multicultural campus: Strategies for
transforming higher education* (pp. 19–29). Walnut Creek, CA:
AltaMira Press.

Vandell, K., and Fishbein, L. (1989). *Women and tenure: The opportunity of a century.* Washington, DC: American Association of
University Women.

Ware, L. (2000). People of color in the academy: Patterns of discrimination in faculty hiring and retention. *Boston College Third World Law Journal, 20,* 55–76.

Washington, V., and Harvey, W. (1989). *Affirmative rhetoric, negative action: African-American and Hispanic faculty at predominantly white institutions.* ASHE-ERIC Higher Education Report 2. Washington, DC: The George Washington University, Graduate School of Education and Human Development.

Washington, V., and Newman, J. (1991). Setting our own agenda: Exploring the meaning of gender disparities among blacks in higher education. *Journal of Negro Education, 60,* 19–35.

Wenzel, S., and Hollenshead, C. (1994, November 10–13). *Tenured women faculty: Reasons for leaving one research university.* Paper presented at the annual meeting of the Association for the Study of Higher Education, Tucson, AZ.

Wiley, N. (1967). The ethnic mobility trap and stratification theory. *Social Problems, 15,* 147–159.

Williams, P. (1991). *The alchemy of race and rights.* Cambridge, MA: Harvard University Press.

Williams, W. (1978). Higher education and minority opportunities. *Howard Law Journal, 21,* 545–557.

Witt, S., and Lovrich, N. (1988). Sources of stress among faculty: Gender differences. *Review of Higher Education, 2,* 269–284.

Wu, F. (1995). Neither black nor white: Asian Americans and affirmative action. *Boston College Third World Law Journal, 15,* 225–284.

Wunsch, M. (1993). Mentoring probationary women academics. *Studies in Higher Education, 18,* 349–362.

Wyche, K., and Graves, S. (1992). Minority women in academia: Access and barriers to professional participation. *Psychology of Women Quarterly, 16,* 429–437.

Yen, A. (1996). A statistical analysis of Asian Americans and the affirmative action hiring of law school faculty. *Asian Law Journal, 3,* 39–54.

Yoder, J. (1985). An academic woman as a token: A case study. *Journal of Social Issues, 41,* 61–72.

Young, D. (1996). Two steps removed: The paradox of diversity discourse for women of color in law teaching. *Berkeley Women's Law Journal, 11,* 270–289.

Young, J. (1984). Black women faculty in academia: Strategies for career leadership development. *Educational and Psychological Research, 4,* 133–145.

NAME INDEX

A

Aguilar, M., 39
Aguirre, A., Jr., 1, 12, 15, 32, 38, 40, 44, 48, 61, 64, 67, 69, 76, 88
Allaie, Y., 28
Allen, W., 82
Alpert, D., 61
Anderson, J., 28, 31
Andrews, S., 45, 46
Arce, C., 51, 52
Armstrong, T., 87
Astin, H., 32, 60, 64, 71, 80
Asunka, K., 45
Austin, A., 26, 27, 42
Ayer, M., 41, 71

B

Bagaka's, J., 87
Banks, W., 47, 67, 70
Barbezat, D., 61
Bartlett, R., 12
Bayer, A., 64
Bell, D., 19, 24, 32, 49, 50, 69
Bellas, M., 53, 61
Belman, D., 65
Bensimon, E., 22, 57
Bentley, R., 12, 13, 33
Berglund, P., 69
Bernstein, A., 3, 42
Billard, L., 1, 33
Blackburn, R., 12, 13, 27, 33, 44, 58, 83
Blackwell, J., 81
Bloom, A., 22, 26
Bogart, K., 12
Bognanno, M., 62
Boli, J., 23
Bressan, S., 12
Brinson, J., 80, 81
Brodie, J., 83
Bromberg, M., 32
Bronstein, P., 52, 53, 54
Brooks, R., 32
Brown, D., 52
Buchen, I., 32, 88
Bunzel, J., 33

C

Caalasanti, T., 87
Cadet, N., 12, 13, 36

Cahalan, M., 64
Cameron, K., 28
Carroll, C., 44
Carter, D., 1, 67
Carter, H., 70, 80
Chaffee, E., 24
Chamberlain, M., 41
Chatman, J., 53
Chepyator-Thomson, J., 32, 71
Chew, P., 15
Ching, Y., 87
Chused, R., 12
Clark, B., 24, 27
Clark, S., 70
Cock, J., 3, 42
Cohen, A., 30
Contreras, A. R., 57, 72, 83
Conway, J., 75
Copeland, J., 31
Corcoran, M., 59, 70
Cortese, A., 5, 80
Cox, T., 35, 54
Creamer, E., 59
Cross, J., 41, 60
Cullen, D. L., 80
Culp, J., 39

D
Darden, J., 87
Davis, D., 45, 60, 71
de los Santos, A., 80
Dejoie, C., 44
Delgado, R., 35, 50
DeLoach, W., 12
Denton, M., 41
Des Jarlais, C., 41, 70, 72
Dey, E., 58
Dickey, C., 80, 81
Dill, D., 23
DiNitto, D., 39, 59
Douthitt, R., 12
Dovidio, J., 48, 49, 61
D'Souza, D., 26
Duane, J., 15, 41

E
Edgert, P., 33
Elmore, C., 44, 83

Epps, E., 39, 82
Ervin, D., 63, 69
Ettington, D., 28
Everett, K., 12
Exum, W., 42, 44, 54, 60, 67, 69, 70, 72

F
Farmer, J., 26
Feagin, J., 82
Field, H., 27
Fields, C., 1, 67
Finkel, S., 14, 68
Finkelstein, M., 1, 30, 64
Firsirotu, M., 28
Fishbein, L., 1
Fitzpatrick, W., 30
Fontaine, D., 60
Ford, D., 64
Franklin, C., 39
Freeman, R., 65, 68

G
Gallant, M., 41, 60
Gamson, Z., 26, 27
Garcia, E., 67
Garza, H., 48
Gattiker, U., 32
Gemmill, G., 41
Giles, W., 27
Gmelch, W., 30, 58, 59
Golbe, D., 65
Golden, M., 80
Gonzales, A., 32, 88
Gose, B., 77, 78
Grandbois, G., 45, 46
Granger, M., 35
Graves, S., 42, 43, 70
Gray, M., 83
Greene, L., 43
Greenlee, S., 60
Grillo, T., 44
Grunig, L., 83
Gummer, B., 1, 75
Gutek, B., 32

H
Hagedorn, L., 63
Hain, B., 1

Haines, A., 44
Halcon, J., 2, 54, 69, 70, 72
Hall, R., 39
Haney-Lopez, I., 71
Haniff, N., 82
Hanson, D., 26
Harris, C., 87
Harrison, D., 12
Harvey, W., 39, 48
Hayes, M., 1
Heilman, M., 2
Henry, M., 41, 60
Henry, W., 39
Hensel, N., 61, 68, 75
Hernandez, A., 40, 44
Hewlett, S., 12
Heywood, J., 65
Higgerson, M. and R., 1, 75
Hill, M., 28, 30
Hirano-Nakanishi, M., 31
Hixson, V., 63
Hofstede, G., 23
Hollenshead, C., 41
Hollon, C., 41
Hu-DeHart, E., 52
Hughes, J., 50

I
Ibarra, H., 54
Imani, N., 82
Irvine, J., 78

J
Jackson, C., l, 80
Jarrell, R., 19
Jencks, C., 24
Jevons, M., 20
Johnsrud, L., 1, 41, 42, 43, 67, 70, 72
Johnston, W., 75
Jolicoeur, P., 28
Jones, J., 28
Jordan, C., 39
Jordan, K., 75
Josey, E., 32, 88
Justus, J., 80

K

Kang, J., 87
Keller, G., 21
Kelly, J., 61
Kerr, C., 22
Kimball, R., 26
King, S., 32, 71
Knater, R., 50
Kottler, J., 80, 81
Kuh, G., 23
Kulis, S., 87
Kupenda, A., 87

L

La Belle, T., 82
Langton, N., 63
Larwood, L., 32
Lawler, A., 26
Lawrence, J., 27, 58
Lee, C., 87
Levine, A., 31
Locke, E., 30
Lorenz, G., 1
Lovrich, N., 28, 30, 31, 59, 68
Luna, G., 61, 80

M

Macilwain, C., 26
Magner, D., 12, 77
Malveaux, J., 32, 78
Mangan, K., 21, 71
Maple, S., 53, 55
Maran, R., 50
Margolis, E., 39
Martinez, R., 40, 44, 67, 69
Martins, L., 50
Matthews, C., 80
Maxson, J., 1
Mazingo, S., 80
McCarthy, M., 19
McCombs, H., 32, 60
McConnell, R., 24
McCormick, T., 80, 81
McKay, N., 39, 70
McMillen, L., 58, 80
McNeer, E., 80
Megdal, S., 61

Mellow, G., 33, 39
Menges, R., 42, 44, 60, 67, 69, 70, 72
Merritt, D., 41, 53
Meta, L., 28
Meyer, J., 23
Milem, J., 32, 80
Milliken, F., 50
Mindiola, T., 67
Montero-Sieburth, M., 43, 61, 72
Mooney, C., 58
Moore, K., 50, 51, 54
Moore, W., 66
Morgan, J., 80
Mortimer, K., 24
Moses, Y., 64
Moy, M., 15
Murray, J., 31
Myers, S., 81
Myers, S., Jr., 87

N
Nakanishi, D., 15
Nettles, M., 65
Newman, J., 76
Nichols, I., 80
Niemann, Y., 48, 49, 61, 87
Nieves-Squires, S., 42, 60
Nixon, H., 39
Nkomo, S., 35, 54
Norman, K. and J., 80

O
O'Brien, E., 1, 67
Olivas, M., 78
Olsen, D., 72
Olswang, S., 14, 68
Ortiz, B., 12
Ortiz, F., 81
Oslen, D., 53, 55
Ottinger, C., 1

P
Park, S., 39, 54
Parson, L., 41, 70
Parson, L. A., 15
Patitu, C. L., 1, 32, 39, 44, 45, 48, 59
Patton, J., 77

Pavel, D. M., 64, 87
Payne, T., 87
Pearson, C., 40
Pearson, D., 28, 31
Perna, L., 65
Peterson, M., 24, 27, 28
Pfeffer, J., 63
Phillips, M.-C., 59, 68
Plata, M., 80
Plater, W., 21, 26, 58
Pounder, D., 61
Powell, M., 32

R
Raja, S., 1
Ransom, M., 61
Rausch, D., 12, 40, 69, 70
Reed, L., 12
Reed, R., 32, 88
Reskin, B., 41, 53
Reyes, M., 2, 54, 69, 70, 72
Rice, R., 24
Rich, H., 28
Rickard, S., 26
Riesman, D., 24
Riger, S., 1, 14
Roberts, D., 26
Robin, H. and S., 61
Robinson, A., 43
Rodriguez, G., 78
Romero, M., 39
Rosenblum, G. and B., 53
Russell, J., 53
Russell, S., 65, 69

S
Sadao, K., 1, 43
Sanders, K., 33, 39
Sandler, B., 39
Sands, R., 15, 41, 76
Schadt, D., 45, 46
Scheff, T., 19, 20
Schiele, J., 43
Schneider, A., 32, 77
Schomberg, S., 26
Seidman, E., 66
Seiler, R., 28

Shavlik, D., 40
Shaw, H., 87
She, N., 69
Shropshire, K., 54
Sikula, R., 1
Simeone, A., 12, 13
Singh, K., 43
Skinner, R., 64
Smart, J., 32
Smith, C., 53
Smith, D., 78
Smith, E., 28, 31, 58
Smith, J., 87
Smith, P., 20, 21, 22, 30, 31
Sowers-Hoag, K., 12
Spencer, M., 24, 28
Stage, F., 53, 55
Stassen, M., 32, 78, 80
Stecklein, J., 1
Steers, R., 53
Stein, J., 64
Steward, R., 72
Stewart, P., 23, 28
Stokes, J., 1
Sullivan, M., 1
Sykes, C., 26

T
Tack, M. W., 1, 32, 39, 44, 45, 48, 59
Takagi, D., 15
Takaki, R., 78
Thomas, B., 63
Thomas, G., 23, 45
Tierney, W., 22, 23, 24, 57
Tippiconnic, M., 64
Toth, E., 41, 60, 70, 71
Touchton, J., 40
Toutkoushian, R., 53, 61
Turner, C., 87
Turner, L., 12, 15, 64

V
Valverde, L., 32
Vandell, K., 1
Vera, H., 82

W
Walker, V., 78
Ward, C., 82
Ware, L., 50
Washington, W., 39, 48, 76
Watkins, B., 69
Wenzel, S., 40
White, F., 30
White, T., 27
Wiley, E., 83
Wiley, N., 48
Wilke, P., 30
Wilkins, R., 81
Williams, P., 82
Williams, W., 52
Williams-Green, J., 43
Witt, E., 23
Witt, S., 59, 68
Wu, F., 87
Wunsch, M., 42, 80
Wyche, K., 42, 43, 70

Y
Yen, A., 15
Yoder, J., 50, 69
Young, D., 44
Young, J., 81

Z
Zey-Ferrell, M., 63
Zeytinoglu, U., 41

SUBJECT INDEX

A

Academia: competitive marketplace and, 20–22; hierarchical relationships in, 24; lifestyle of, 23; perceived as multicultural, 35; popular image of, 19–20. *See also* Academic workplace; Higher education

Academic advisors, women faculty as, 73

Academic culture: academic workplace and, 27–31; diversity in, 79–81; and professional goals, 23–26, 28

Academic workplace: allocation of responsibilities in, 40–41; ascribed roles for minority/women faculty in, 50–52; autonomy and independence in, 28; barriers to minority faculty in, 46–50; elite system in, 39; minority faculty as threat in, 52–53; minority faculty's perceptions of, 44–45; organizational fit and, 53–56; satisfaction/dissatisfaction with, 28–31; stressors in, 58–60; unequal opportunities in, 40–42; unreceptive environment for women/minority faculty in, 1–2; women faculty's perceptions of, 40–44; women as potential threats in, 50, 52–53. *See also* Workplace diversity; Workplace stress

Administrative work, 27

Affirmative action initiatives, 1, 2, 12, 32–33; salary differentials and, 61–62; tokenism and, 73

American Indian faculty, 87

Asian American faculty, 87; discrimination and, 15; increase in, 76

B

Black faculty: job satisfaction of, 45; networking and, 80; representation of, 75–77; workplace perceptions of, 47–48

C

Committee responsibilities: gender and, 40–41, 42; minority faculty and, 48, 73; perceived as busy work, 27

Community of scholars, 24

Community services, faculty's role in, 26–27

Consultation activities, 26

Culture, defined, 23

D

Decision making, women faculty's participation in, 40–44

Diversity. *See* Workplace diversity

Doctoral degrees: comparative statistics on, 9–12, 13–14; minority salary and, 65–66; women with, 75–76, 77

E

Ethnic mobility trap, 48

F

Faculty rank: comparative statistics on, 5–9; professorial, male dominance of, 32–33

Faculty representation, comparative statistics on, 2–5, 9–12, 13–16
Feminist studies, 52–53

G

Gender discrimination, 52, 60; in salary, 61–64; in workplace, 42

H

Higher education institutions: conservative versus liberal humanist
image of, 22; hierarchical classification of, 24; women's increased
enrollment in, 1, 75–76; women's traditional subservient role
in, 50

I

Institutional barriers: biased reward system as, 66–69; for minority
faculty, 44–45, 46–40; and organizational fit, 53–56; to professional socialization, 41, 42, 57–61, 69–72; role assignments as,
50–53; and salary differentials, 61–66; for women faculty, 40–44

J

Job content, stressors in, 58
Job satisfaction: of black faculty, 45; extrinsic/intrinsic workplace
features and, 28–31; solo status and, 48–50
Joint academic appointments, 67–68, 70

L

Latino faculty: increase in, 76; research focus on, 86; role perceptions of, 44–45; specialized "Chicano roles" for, 51–52
Leadership roles, race and, 44

M

Mentoring activities, 80–81
Minority faculty: biased reward system and, 66–68, 71–72; with
doctoral degrees, earnings of, 65–66; leadership roles and, 44;
model citizen role of, 50, 51; peripheral and segmented status of,
53–54, 83; professional socialization of, 42–44, 84–86; quality of
life issues for, 44–45; service activities and, 43–44, 47; solo status
of, 48–50; tenure and, 67–68; unreceptive academic environment
for, 1–2; use of term, 86–87; tokenism and, 45, 53–54, 72–73;
white students' biased perceptions of, 82–83
Minority faculty representation, 15–16, 75–77; affirmative action
and, 32–33; faculty perception of, 33–36; female, comparative
statistics on, 2–3; male, comparative statistics on, 3–5
Minority women faculty: decision–making participation of, 40; dual
effects of racism and sexism on, 43; professional socialization of,
42–44; service activities and, 43–44; symbolic roles of, 43
Multicultural studies, 52–53

N

Negotiated identities, 72–73

O

Organizational fit, 53–56, 83–84
Organizational stressors, 58

P

Professional goals, academic culture and, 23–26, 28
Professional socialization: institutional barriers to, 41, 42, 57–61; of
    minority women faculty, 42–44; research and, 70–71; service and
    teaching demands and, 70; social isolation and, 69–70; workplace
    environment and, 45, 58–59
Professorial rank, 5, 7–9; white male dominance of, 32–33
Proposition 209 (California), 32

Q

Quality of life issues, for minority faculty, 44–45

R

Racial bias, 43, 52, 60; of white students, 82–83
Research and publication, 54, 55; academia's focus on, 20–21;
    changing marketplace and, 24–26; minority/feminist, delegit-
    imization of, 70–71; of women faculty, 42; workplace stress
    and, 59
Reward system bias, 66–69
Role entrapment, 50–53
Role interests, and organizational fit, 55

S

Salary differentials: affirmative action and, 61–62; gender and,
    61–64; minority status and, 64–66
Service activities: as barrier to career advancement, 47; and black
    minority faculty, 47; demands of, 70; and minority faculty, 43–44;
    and organizational fit, 83
Social isolation, 69–70
Solo status, impact of, 48–50, 61

T

Teaching assignments: professional socialization and, 70; stress
    and, 59–60
Tenure: marriage and childbearing and, 68–69; of minority faculty,
    67–68
Tokenism, 53–54, 72–73

W

White male faculty: in academic culture, 81–82; as gatekeepers, 51;
    as professors, dominance of, 32–33; representation of, 2–4

Women faculty: biased reward system and, 68–69, 71–72; decision–making participation of, 40; with doctoral degrees, 75–76; marginalization of, 39–40, 40–44; marriage and childbearing and, 68–69; peripheral and segmented status of, 53–54; professional socialization of, 42–44, 84–86; representation and comparative statistics, 2–3, 12–15, 75–77; unreceptive academic environment and, 1–2; workplace issues for, 40–41. *See also* Minority women faculty

Workplace diversity, 81–84; academic culture and, 79–81; benefits of, 75; affirmative action and, 31–36; initiatives, faculty responses to, 33–36; initiatives, success in, 77–78

Workplace stress, 58–60; discrimination and, 60; professional socialization and, 58–59; teaching load and, 59–60

ASHE-ERIC HIGHER EDUCATION REPORTS

The mission of the Educational Resources Information Center (ERIC) system is to improve American education by increasing and facilitating the use of educational research and information on practice in the activities of learning, teaching, educational decision making, and research, wherever and whenever these activities take place.

Since 1983, the ASHE-ERIC Higher Education Report Series has been published in cooperation with the Association for the Study of Higher Education (ASHE). Starting in 2000, the series is published by Jossey-Bass in conjunction with the ERIC Clearinghouse on Higher Education.

Each monograph is the definitive analysis of a tough higher education problem, based on thorough research of pertinent literature and institutional experiences. Topics are identified by a national survey. Noted practitioners and scholars are then commissioned to write the reports, with experts providing critical reviews of each manuscript before publication.

Eight monographs (10 before 1985) in the ASHE-ERIC Higher Education Report series are published each year and are available on individual and subscription bases. To order, use the order form on the last page of this book.

Qualified persons interested in writing a monograph for the ASHE-ERIC Higher Education Report series are invited to submit a proposal to the National Advisory Board. As the preeminent literature review and issue analysis series in higher education, the Higher Education Reports are guaranteed wide dissemination and national exposure for accepted candidates. Execution of a monograph requires at least a minimal familiarity with the ERIC database, including *Resources in Education* and the current *Index to Journals in Education*. The objective of these reports is to bridge conventional wisdom with practical research.

ADVISORY BOARD

CONSULTING EDITORS AND REVIEW PANEL

Jacques DuBois
Synergy Plus, Inc.

Kassie Freeman
Peabody College

Timothy Gallineau
Buffalo State College

Kenneth C. Green
The Campus Computing Project

Philo A. Hutcheson
Georgia State University

Elizabeth A. Jones
West Virginia University

Toby Milton
Essex Community College

Diana Oblinger
International Business Machines Corporation

Steven Sachs
Northern Virginia Community College

Scott Swail
The College Board

William Tierney
University of Southern California

Susan B. Twombly
University of Kansas

RECENT TITLES

Volume 27 ASHE-ERIC Higher Education Reports

1. The Art and Science of Classroom Assessment: The Missing
   Part of Pedagogy
   Susan M. Brookhart

2. Due Process and Higher Education: A Systemic Approach to
   Fair Decision Making
   Ed Stevens

3. Grading Students' Classroom Writing: Issues and Strategies
   Bruce W. Speck

4. Posttenure Faculty Development: Building a System for
   Faculty Improvement and Appreciation
   Jeffrey W. Alstete

5. Digital Dilemma: Issues of Access, Cost, and Quality in Media-
   Enhanced and Distance Education
   Gerald C. Van Dusen

Volume 26 ASHE-ERIC Higher Education Reports

1. Faculty Workload Studies: Perspectives, Needs, and Future
   Directions
   Katrina A. Meyer

2. Assessing Faculty Publication Productivity: Issues of Equity
   Elizabeth G. Creamer

3. Proclaiming and Sustaining Excellence: Assessment as a
   Faculty Role
   Karen Maitland Schilling and Karl L. Schilling

4. Creating Learning Centered Classrooms: What Does Learning
   Theory Have to Say?
   *Frances K. Stage, Patricia A. Muller, Jillian Kinzie, and
   Ada Simmons*

5. The Academic Administrator and the Law: What Every Dean
   and Department Chair Needs to Know
   J. Douglas Toma and Richard L. Palm

6. The Powerful Potential of Learning Communities: Improving
   Education for the Future
   Oscar T. Lenning and Larry H. Ebbers

7. Enrollment Management for the 21st Century: Institutional
   Goals, Accountability, and Fiscal Responsibility
   Garlene Penn

8. Enacting Diverse Learning Environments: Improving the
   Climate for Racial/Ethnic Diversity in Higher Education
   *Sylvia Hurtado, Jeffrey Milem, Alma Clayton-Pedersen,
   and Walter Allen*

Volume 25 ASHE-ERIC Higher Education Reports

1. A Culture for Academic Excellence: Implementing the Quality Principles in Higher Education
   Jann E. Freed, Marie R. Klugman, and Jonathan D. Fife

2. From Discipline to Development: Rethinking Student Conduct in Higher Education
   Michael Dannells

3. Academic Controversy: Enriching College Instruction Through Intellectual Conflict
   David W. Johnson, Roger T. Johnson, and Karl A. Smith

4. Higher Education Leadership: Analyzing the Gender Gap
   Luba Chliwniak

5. The Virtual Campus: Technology and Reform in Higher Education
   Gerald C. Van Dusen

6. Early Intervention Programs: Opening the Door to Higher Education
   Robert H. Fenske, Christine A. Geranios, Jonathan E. Keller, and David E. Moore

7. The Vitality of Senior Faculty Members: Snow on the Roof—Fire in the Furnace
   Carole J. Bland and William H. Bergquist

8. A National Review of Scholastic Achievement in General Education: How Are We Doing and Why Should We Care?
   Steven J. Osterlind

Volume 24 ASHE-ERIC Higher Education Reports

1. Tenure, Promotion, and Reappointment: Legal and Administrative Implications
   Benjamin Baez and John A. Centra

2. Taking Teaching Seriously: Meeting the Challenge of Instructional Improvement
   Michael B. Paulsen and Kenneth A. Feldman

3. Empowering the Faculty: Mentoring Redirected and Renewed
   Gaye Luna and Deborah L. Cullen

4. Enhancing Student Learning: Intellectual, Social, and Emotional Integration
   Anne Goodsell Love and Patrick G. Love

5. Benchmarking in Higher Education: Adapting Best Practices to Improve Quality
   Jeffrey W. Alstete

6. Models for Improving College Teaching: A Faculty Resource
   Jon E. Travis

7. Experiential Learning in Higher Education: Linking Classroom and Community
   Jeffrey A. Cantor

8. Successful Faculty Development and Evaluation: The Complete Teaching Portfolio
   John P. Murray

Volume 23 ASHE-ERIC Higher Education Reports

1. The Advisory Committee Advantage: Creating an Effective Strategy for Programmatic Improvement
   Lee Teitel

2. Collaborative Peer Review: The Role of Faculty in Improving College Teaching
   Larry Keig and Michael D. Waggoner

3. Prices, Productivity, and Investment: Assessing Financial Strategies in Higher Education
   Edward P. St. John

4. The Development Officer in Higher Education: Toward an Understanding of the Role
   Michael J. Worth and James W. Asp II

5. Measuring Up: The Promises and Pitfalls of Performance Indicators in Higher Education
   Gerald Gaither, Brian P. Nedwek, and John E. Neal

6. A New Alliance: Continuous Quality and Classroom Effectiveness
   Mimi Wolverton

7. Redesigning Higher Education: Producing Dramatic Gains in Student Learning
   Lion F. Gardiner

8. Student Learning Outside the Classroom: Transcending Artificial Boundaries
   George D. Kuh, Katie Branch Douglas, Jon P. Lund, and Jackie Ramin-Gyurnek

Back Issue/Subscription Order Form

Copy or detach and send to:
Jossey-Bass, 350 Sansome Street, San Francisco CA 94104-1342

Call or fax toll free!
Phone 888-378-2537 6AM-5PM PST; Fax 800-605-2665

Individual reports:	Please send me the following reports at $24 each (Important: please include series initials and issue number, such as AEHE 27:1)

1. AEHE _____

_____

_____

$ _____ Total for individual reports

$ _____ Shipping charges (for individual reports *only;* subscriptions are exempt from shipping charges): Up to $30, add $5^{50} • $30^{01}–$50, add $6^{50} $50^{01}–$75, add $8 • $75^{01}–$100, add $10 • $100^{01}–$150, add $12 Over $150, call for shipping charge

Subscriptions Please ❑ start ❑ renew my subscription to *ASHE-ERIC Higher Education Reports* for the year <u>2000</u> at the following rate (8 issues):   U.S. $144   Canada: $169   All others: $174

Please ❑ start my subscription to *ASHE-ERIC Higher Education Reports* for the year <u>2001</u> at the following rate (8 issues): U.S. $108   Canada: $133   All others: $138

NOTE: Subscriptions are for the calendar year only. Subscriptions begin with Report 1 of the year indicated above.

$ _____ Total individual reports and subscriptions (Add appropriate sales tax for your state for individual reports. No sales tax on U.S. subscriptions. Canadian residents, add GST for subscriptions and individual reports.)

❑ Payment enclosed (U.S. check or money order only)

❑ VISA, MC, AmEx, Discover Card # _____ Exp. date _____

Signature _____ Day phone _____

❑ Bill me (U.S. institutional orders only. Purchase order required.)

Purchase order #_____

Federal Tax ID 1355   GST 89102-8052

Name _____

Address _____

_____

Phone_____ E-mail _____

For more information about Jossey-Bass, visit our Web site at:
www.josseybass.com   **PRIORITY CODE = ND1**